# Justice Sandra Day O'Connor

# Justice
# Sandra Day
# O'Connor

## JUDITH BENTLEY

Julian Messner    New York

JULIAN MESSNER and colophon are trademarks of
Simon & Schuster, Inc.

10 9 8 7 6 5 4 3 2

Manufactured in the United States of America

Design by Stanley S. Drak

Frontispiece: Don B. Stevenson/Mesa Tribune

Library of Congress Cataloging in Publication Data

Bentley, Judith.
Justice Sandra Day O'Connor.

Bibliography: p.
Includes index.
Summary: A biography of the former Arizona state senator and judge who
in 1981 became the first woman ever appointed a justice of the United
States Supreme Court.
    1. O'Connor, Sandra Day, 1930–    —Juvenile
literature.  2. Judges—United States—Biography—Juvenile
literature.  [1. O'Connor, Sandra Day,
    1930–    2. Judges.  3. United States. Supreme
Court—Biography]  I. Title.

KF8745.025B46   1983      347.73'2634 [B] [92] 83-42786
        ISBN 0-671-45809-4        347.3073534 [B]

*To all the women
who paved the way*

# Acknowledgments

Telling the story of someone's life requires interviewing the people who know her. Sandra O'Connor has made many friends in her life; all those I asked were willing to share their part of her story. Their names are listed in the Sources at the end of this book.

Most of all I would like to thank Ada Mae and Harry A. Day, her parents, and Alan and Barbara Day for their reminiscences and hospitality at the Lazy B Ranch in Arizona. Ann Day Alexander also freely shared her family's history. I would like to thank Justice O'Connor herself for taking time from her first year on the Court to grant me an interview.

Also helpful were Mary Lou Bessette, assistant to the managing editor, and Marcy Bagley, librarian, at the *Arizona Republic*; Laura Kramer, historian at the Radford School; Kay Daley, Stanford Alumni Association editor; Betsy T. Strawderman, assistant curator, Supreme Court of the United States; and the staff of the Arizona Room of the Phoenix Public Library.

Jane Steltenpohl, senior editor at Julian Messner, suggested this book as well as the first one I wrote, and I am grateful to her for her guidance and patience.

Last (aren't spouses always last?) I thank Allen Bentley for toting home Supreme Court opinions and serving as my in-house counsel, not to mention everything else he does as supportive husband and full-time father.

# Contents

Introduction / xi

1 Arizona Pioneers / 1

2 City and Country / 11

3 Becoming a Lawyer / 19

4 Family First / 33

5 Excelling in Politics / 51

6 The Iron Judge / 65

7 A President's Promise / 77

8 Her Honor, Justice O'Connor / 95

Sources / 117

Index / 121

# Introduction

"I do solemnly swear that I will support and defend the Constitution of the United States"—a simple, short oath but one never before taken by a woman justice of the Supreme Court of the United States. The oath and the position had been denied to women for almost two hundred years. Both were being given this sunny afternoon in September 1981 to a woman in a short black robe with a lavender collar peeping through.

"I marveled that an event so steeped in tradition would consume only a few minutes," wrote one observer. "She spoke no words, except her oath, which was followed by a smile at the President and a 'Welcome' from the Chief Justice. Yet with this simple ceremony she began walking where no woman had ever walked before."

Sandra Day O'Connor was indeed unique. She was the right person at the right historical moment. She was ranch bred, Stanford educated, seasoned in Arizona politics, and experienced as a judge when a Republican President decided to nominate a woman to the Supreme Court.

Other women had paved the way. Myra Bradwell appealed to the U.S. Supreme Court to be allowed to practice law in Illinois in 1872, but the Court said "God designed the sexes to occupy different spheres of action," and "it belongs to men to make, apply, and execute the law." (Iowa had already allowed a woman, Belle Mansfield, to practice law in 1869.)

Florence Allen was the first woman named a federal judge, in 1934, and she sought a nomination to the Supreme Court, but she was forty years too early. Shirley Hufstedler was reported to be President Jimmy Carter's choice for the Court, but he never had a vacancy to fill there.

But Sandra Day O'Connor succeeded. She was a woman who had put family first but managed a remarkable career, too, a woman of integrity, intelligence, and charm. She had faced traditional obstacles: the law schools' reluctance to admit women then, hiring discrimination, practicing law while she had young children at home, and steering bills through the state senate while helping her sons pack for summer camp. She was a determined woman who knew her own mind and made her own way when the way for women was not very clear.

The ceremony was the same as it had been for the 101 justices who preceded her. At a few minutes past two o'clock President Ronald Reagan and Sandra O'Connor entered the ornate marble and mahogany courtroom from opposite sides. O'Connor was escorted to a ceremonial chair while the eight other justices stood silently at the large, curved, elevated bench. After the clerk read the commission signed by the President, Chief Justice Warren Burger called O'Connor up to the bench and administered the oath. She was helped on with her robe, and then she took her place at the far end of the bench where the newest justice always sits.

"She looked around, saw the family, and locked her eyes right into ours," said her brother Alan Day. "That's when the tears started falling."

# 1

# Arizona Pioneers

Five-year-old Sandra Day was on her way to live with her Wilkey grandparents in El Paso, Texas, for the school year. Her father, Harry A. Day, was driving the Chevrolet. Her mother, Ada Mae Wilkey Day, talked about the brick house on Tularosa Avenue, the school Sandra would go to—the Radford School for Girls—and possibly "of cabbages and kings."

Sandra at five had dark, short hair, dark eyebrows, and a way of looking straight at you. She was intelligent and already knew how to read. Her parents were sad to be losing the company of their first child, but they knew she would be in loving hands. There was simply no suitable school near their isolated ranch.

Driving to El Paso to visit the Wilkeys or to Pasadena, California, to visit the Day relatives was not new to Sandra. She often slept on the back seat of the car. But most of her first five years had been spent on a set from a Wild West dream—the Lazy B Ranch.

The Lazy B covers some 170,000 acres of cactus and greasewood in southeastern Arizona. Six thousand head of cattle roam from the Gila River basin to desert high country on the Arizona–New Mexico border. Some of the land, a house, corrals, outbuildings, and several 20-foot windmills—the kind they don't make anymore—have belonged to the Day family since the ranch was established in the 1880s.

The day Sandra was born, March 26, 1930, in El Paso, her father, Harry, was in federal court in Tucson engaged in a dispute with a former partner over the division of the ranch's property. The Lazy B's future was somewhat precarious at the time. Harry questioned whether his wife, Ada Mae, really wanted to bring a month-old baby back to a four-room adobe house with no plumbing, no electricity, no running water or gas, and four cowboys bunking on the front porch.

As Ada Mae recalls it, she didn't have much choice. "I missed Harry, and the cowboys needed me. I had to love him, or think I did, to move out here."

The ranch began when Arizona was still a territory. Henry Clay Day, Harry's father, grew up in Vermont, but at the age of twenty-one he went west and made "quite a little fortune" dabbling in lumber and real estate in Wichita, Kansas. He married Alice Edith Hilton, which led him to an opportunity to invest his fortune.

Sandra's grandmother Alice had lived with a

Judge Fisher's family in Wichita since her parents died when she was in her teens. The Fishers had a son, Lane, who had been with the army in the Southwest, probably fighting Indians.

Captain Fisher had some stories to tell the adventurous Henry. There in the territory of Arizona, he related, "was this wide open area with nothing on it. It had water in the Gila River and up in a side valley. It was good grass country, and it looked good to raise cattle on." The land was all public domain, and anyone could turn cattle loose there.

Henry—called H.C.—was willing, so he and Lane Fisher formed a partnership. H.C. put up the money and Fisher went to Mexico and bought about six thousand head of cattle at ten dollars a head. He drove them back across the border and turned them loose on the range in the area that became the Day ranch. The cattle came with a brand, a capital B lying on its side—ᗺ. The brand gave the ranch its name: the Lazy B.

H.C. and Alice moved into an adobe house on the ranch, on cultivated land by the Gila River. They arrived from Kansas soon after the Southern Pacific Railroad was completed through Lordsburg, New Mexico, some 25 miles away, in 1882. The Days weren't sure they planned to stay, but when a big flood washed out their first house (and carried away the grand piano), they decided to build another home on higher ground. There in 1898 Sandra's father Harry was born, their fifth and last child.

Flash floods were not the only hazard in the

early days of the ranch. Most of the Apache Indians, who had roamed the area for years, had been persuaded to live on the San Carlos reservation in Arizona. But not all accepted the reservation life. A leader named Geronimo and a band of renegade Apaches were attacking settlers and ranchers in the area. The Days escaped harm but lost forty-five horses to the raiders. After Geronimo surrendered in 1886, more settlers began moving into Arizona, and the territory moved slowly toward statehood.

Neighbors were still scarce around the Lazy B. Duncan, Arizona, the nearest town, was twenty miles away. The main road connecting Duncan with Lordsburg, New Mexico, was eight miles from what is now the headquarters of the ranch. Because there were few people and very few children, a proper education was hard to come by. H.C. built a one-room schoolhouse for the local children, known as the Day District School. The teacher lived with the family. But there was no high school within easy traveling distance.

The search for a better education eventually caused the Days to leave the ranch. When the two oldest children reached high school age, one went to Topeka, Kansas, and the other to Santa Ana, California, to attend school. When the youngest were finishing elementary school, the family decided to move to Pasadena, California. There young Harry finished high school and decided he wanted to go on to Stanford, the new university of the West.

Word came, however, that the ranch was in

trouble. To keep it going, H.C. had taken in two brothers as partners and sold them a one-third interest. After he died in 1921, followed by Alice in 1926, the ranch was in bad shape and the partners were out of money. Harry decided to give up his plans for Stanford and return to the ranch, though his older sister Eleanor declared it wasn't worth saving.

For the next ten years Harry spent a lot of time in court, dividing the ranch's property among the partners and the estate. But he also set about making the ranch prosper again. A key to its future, and his, was a cattle trade he worked out with Willis Willard Wilkey.

Willis W. Wilkey and his wife Mamie also came from southwestern pioneer families who had prospered in mining and cattle trading. After W.W. and Mamie Scott were married, they moved to Mexico to work with Colonel William Greene at his copper mine and smelter in Cananea. But they were forced to return across the border, with two-year-old Ada Mae, when striking Mexican miners turned on the American families there in 1906.

The Wilkeys opened a store in Duncan, not far from the Lazy B. Because they felt, too, that education was important for their children, they moved to El Paso when they had prospered in the business and in cattle trading on the side. The search for better schools was thus an important theme in the background of both of Sandra's parents.

By the time Ada Mae Wilkey encountered

Harry Day, she was a sophisticated young woman of the Southwest. She had been to Europe at age sixteen on a tour led by her English teacher, and she had graduated from the University of Arizona in Tucson. A soprano vocalist and pianist, she was known in El Paso for her musical talent. She was an educated woman when she met a self-made man in the making.

"My father likes to say he met my mother when he went to buy some bulls from her father and she was part of the deal," Sandra relates. "That is not true, of course."

The complete story is that Ada Mae and Harry met as children and again as teenagers, but it was not until Harry came back from California to take over the ranch that he really noticed Ada Mae. He had worked out a trade with her father, W.W., to get new bulls for the ranch, and the two men went together to Big Spring, Texas, to inspect the bulls. They took the train back to El Paso.

"She [Ada Mae] was sitting out there in the car when we got off the train. She kinda smiled at me, and that was it," Harry recalls. "I thought, 'My God, that little girl I knew up there has really matured.'"

A long-distance courtship followed, with letters back and forth between the ranch and El Paso and train rides for visits. When that became tiresome, they eloped one night in September 1928 to Las Cruces, New Mexico. When Harry brought Ada Mae back to the ranch on which he was born, neither of them was really used to that kind of life.

They had spent many years in cities, he in Pasadena and she in El Paso. "But I thought if other people could do it, I was sure I could," Harry said. "I just liked the wide open life."

The wide open life was important in the formation of Sandra Day's character. The home she was brought to in 1930 was a struggling ranch, managed by a man dedicated to making a go of it and a woman dedicated to him. But Mrs. Day also intended to rear her daughter in tune with the larger world and its culture. She was a woman who dressed fashionably in the middle of the desert and possessed the social graces, which she would pass on to her daughters.

The main activity for Sandra was reading. Mrs. Day read to her by the hour, starting at an early age, from anything she could find: books from the Book of the Month Club, stories from the *Saturday Evening Post*, excerpts from the *Book of Knowledge* and *National Geographic*. In time, through mail order and purchases made on trips, the ranch developed its own library. "Our main entertainment was reading," Mrs. Day recalls.

For news the Days depended on the *Los Angeles Times*, the *Wall Street Journal*, and *Time* magazine, all of which came by mail. Sandra was to say later that she had enjoyed following the career of Clare Boothe Luce (wife of *Time* editor Henry R. Luce) and considers her a remarkable woman.

To teach Sandra to read, Ada Mae used the Calvert method, a popular series of lessons for children in remote areas, which one subscribed to by mail. Sandra had no playmates or siblings when she was very young. The inhabitants of her world were cowboys like Bug Quinn and Claude Tippett, horses, cows, and for a time, cats.

Her father described the cat phase: "Sandra took to kittens one year, and they really multiplied. She used to feed them off the back porch, and they were always underfoot. You know the sound kittens made—*yaoryll*—they'd make that when you stepped on them as you went out the door. So when Sandra was away once, I rounded a bunch of them up and took them out to High Lonesome, a windmill we have out on the range, and let them go. Feral cats can survive in an area like this.

"Sandra didn't seem to catch on that they were gone. Then one day I took her over to the windmill with me, and one of the cats came bounding up to the truck. 'Why that's my little Suzy,' she said, scooping her up and a few more that came running, and then scolded me roundly for what I had done."

Wherever Harry went, Sandra followed if she could—learning to ride a horse, drive a pickup truck, shoot jackrabbits, fix windmills, repair fences, put out salt, and tend sick cattle. From following her father around and learning what he did, Sandra learned practicality and self-reliance. If the car stalled or the pipes burst, you fixed it yourself. You learned to "take care of your own problems and do the best you can."

For diversion she and her mother would go almost anyplace Harry went in a vehicle. Mr. and Mrs. Day socialized with a small group of ranchers and miners at the hotel in Lordsburg, leaving Sandra in the care of the bellhop while they danced or chatted.

The ranch was never fancy when Sandra was growing up there. A separate bunkhouse for the cowboys and indoor plumbing for the Days' house were added when she was seven. Food was kept cold in an icebox with ice transported from Lordsburg. The times Harry came back with a 300-pound block of ice were occasions for celebration. Because the entire block wouldn't fit inside the icebox, some of it was kept covered in a tub and the rest went into lemonade and homemade ice cream. The occasion was special in a climate where the sun beats down most of the year and the water coming out of the tap is usually warm.

The 1930s were hard times at the ranch as well as elsewhere in the nation. Drought made grass more sparse than usual, and the cattle never fattened. "I was scared," Harry Day remembers. "I kept five hundred dollars in a safe-deposit box in case we had to leave here." Finally, the federal government stepped in, killing the sickly cows but paying Mr. Day twelve dollars a head for them. The government also paid as much as twenty dollars a head for the ones worth shipping to market.

Much as the Days and ranch life had to offer in

the way of a practical education, the ranch was isolated. Its location limited the schooling available to a bright child. So in 1935 Sandra was on her way to start kindergarten at Radford. There she was to find academic stimulation, companionship, and a loving "second mother."

# 2

# City and Country

El Paso was a bustling railroad and cattle-trading city when Sandra arrived in 1935. Her Grandfather Wilkey conducted his cattle brokering at the St. Regis Hotel. The houses in town were all made of brick, including the one on Tularosa Avenue, where her grandparents lived.

Grandmother Wilkey was a very strong-willed, assertive woman in a family of energetic women. She took care of all the grandchildren as they came to El Paso for school, and nothing fazed her. Sandra recalls that her grandmother was very young when she lived with her—like a second mother, loving and caring. She was also a good cook and known as the best bridge player in El Paso. She carried on single-handedly after her husband died when Sandra was in the third grade.

Sandra knew she would have at least one good friend at Radford—her cousin Flournoy Davis.

Flournoy was the daughter of Ada Mae's sister Evelyn. The two girls were constant companions and always a contrast: Flournoy with long, blonde braids and Sandra with short, dark hair.

It was good to have an ally. After kindergarten at Radford, Sandra and Flournoy went to a public school, the Crockett School, for first and second grades and then returned to Radford for third grade in the fall of 1937. "The first month or two were just grim," Flournoy remembers, "because we were outsiders. Once we were accepted, the school was just fine."

The Radford School was a girls' school founded in 1910 as the El Paso School for Girls and endowed by Mr. and Mrs. George Radford in 1931. It featured small classes of eight to ten girls and dedicated teachers. It was five miles from town, accessible by the horsecar line or private auto. The girls ate together in a dining room with a different teacher at each table leading discussions.

From all accounts, Sandra's academic record there was a strong one. Her teachers realized she was bright and advanced her a grade. She also joined the Melody Club for music students in the fourth and fifth grades.

Sandra especially remembers a dramatic arts teacher, Miss Fireoved, a graduate of Boston's Emerson School of Oratory, who taught her a lot about speaking in public, a skill she would later put to good use. "We learned a great deal of presence before groups," Flournoy adds, "because we put on lots of productions." Frequently, just before lunch the girls would be assigned a topic to talk about right after lunch. In this way, they learned quickly how to speak extemporaneously.

Sandra's school years were a tug between the ranch and El Paso. She was always homesick. "We missed her terribly, and she missed us," her mother said, "but there was no other way for her to get a good education." Her younger sister Ann remembers feeling that she lived in two different worlds, ranch and city, when she followed a similar path.

Winters (except for vacations) were spent in the city, riding around the neighborhood on Flournoy's bicycle and putting on elaborate plays in the Guynes's garage. (Being slow in learning to ride a bicycle is the only verified delay in Sandra's development.) Once they "borrowed" Aunt Evelyn's good jewelry to use as buried treasure while playing Indians. The treasure was buried all over a vacant lot, and some of it never was recovered.

During the summers Flournoy and Sandra took the train back to the ranch, riding under the supervision of a hostess in the club car. Once there, they enjoyed a playhouse, using gourds for tea settings, and they put on plays for the cowboys on the porch of the bunkhouse. Both girls were avid readers and frequent cardplayers. Sandra was a whiz at games, very fast and very quick, much to Flournoy's dismay.

They rode constantly, usually without saddle or bridle. Frequent destinations were an old swimming hole where they fished with safety-pin hooks and Cottonwood Canyon on the Gila River where ancient Indian tribes had left pictographs. If they strayed too far Sandra knew how to follow the different pasture fences back to the house.

At the end of the summer, Sandra was always reluctant to go back to El Paso, so she would hide. Once she and Flournoy refused to come down from the stock tank, where they were swimming away the vacation. Harry got his lariat and roped them both out.

Whether at school or at home, Sandra's education in practical skills continued. Her father taught her to use a small gauge .22 so she could shoot jackrabbits, prairie dogs, coyotes, rattlesnakes, or Gila monsters—all critters that ate the pasture grass or went after the cattle.

From her mother Sandra learned to cook and organize a meal for a large crowd, as when the family gathered at Christmas. Visitors to the ranch, whether cattle buyers or salesmen, usually stayed for a while, giving the family a chance to get to know them.

"Harry was a wonderful storyteller and conversationalist," Flournoy said, "and he always brought us into the conversation." Later he and Sandra would embark on political discussions that often revealed one to be as opinionated as the other. Sandra was reported to be more liberal than her father, who favored Senator Robert A. Taft and never liked Franklin D. Roosevelt.

By the time Sandra was ten, in 1940, she had a sister Ann, born in 1938, and a brother Alan, born a year later. They were too much younger to be playmates for her and fought with each other instead.

Alan recalls that he was a hell-raiser and that Sandra, who was very straight, usually disapproved when he did things like smoking in the haystack. Although she could be a stern big sister on such occasions, she was also kind and giving, and he speaks of her with genuine admiration. "I have to be fairly on my toes to win her approval," he said, and "that's great."

In later summers, the five Days would climb into the car for a traditional family vacation. They enjoyed a trip to Alaska, a banana boat excursion to Cuba and Honduras, fishing trips in Mexico, cattlemen's conventions, a stay at a beach house in California, and especially a tour of all the state capitals west of the Mississippi River. They climbed to the dome of the capitol building in every state except Texas. "It was always interesting but not always pleasant," Ann relates, when the family got hot and tired.

Her parents remained the main influence in Sandra's early life. Discipline was light, although the threat to "wash out your mouth with soap" was carried out once, to the distaste of Sandra and Flournoy. From her mother, Sandra learned to be gracious and dignified, even under extreme conditions. From her father, she learned common sense and a strong sense of honesty and fair play—the importance of being "able to hold your head up and look people right in the eye." Others tell of both parents' interest in the world, of tremendous curiosity and a desire to get to the bottom of things, which rubbed off on Sandra.

Because she was always homesick in El Paso, the Days decided to enroll Sandra at the local school in Lordsburg for eighth grade. The school was thirty-two miles away and required that the Days meet the school bus on the highway before daylight and after dark in the evening during the winter months. It was not a satisfactory experience, educationally or otherwise. Sandra had no chance to stay after school and no time really to do homework either. The memory predisposed Sandra to disapprove of busing children long distances to school. The next year she returned to Radford.

The year Sandra went to the Lordsburg school she lost her childhood pudginess and grew tall and pretty. Soon she began to be interested in meeting boys, a difficult feat on the ranch or at Radford. So she transferred to coed Austin High School in El Paso. By now she was two years ahead of others her age.

By her friends' account, Sandra did all the normal things teenagers did, had crushes and talked about boys. She was too smart for most of her male classmates, however. As a teenager Sandra seemed reserved and mature and never really rebellious.

"Sandra always knew how to handle herself," said her high school friend Hondey Hill McAlmon in an interview in *McCall's*. "She was in honor classes and was terrific at impromptu speaking . . . . She was never loud or awkward. I was never jealous of her, but I do remember feeling a little inferior. She really could do everything well."

Suddenly high school graduation loomed ahead, and Sandra was the only one in her class who planned to go to college. Her mind was set on Stanford, the school her father had hoped to attend. She was so confident of being accepted and so sure of her preference that she applied to only one school.

Several factors were working against her acceptence, however: she was only sixteen; Austin had neglected to give her a college entrance exam; and thousands of soldiers returning from World War II were competing for the same spots. A friend of her father's doubted she would ever get in (and he *knew* she wouldn't get into the law school when she applied three years later.) Not many girls from out in the boondocks were ever accepted without some kind of pull.

Sandra's pull was her academic record along with her list of extracurricular activities. No doubt she impressed anyone who met her, too, with her poise and seriousness. She was admitted to the university. "We took her up there to Stanford, deposited money in the Bank of America, and taught her how to write a check," her father recalls.

Besides native intelligence, social graces, and encouraging parents, Sandra had a good measure of common sense and self-reliance. Everyone who knows her emphasizes the importance of life on the ranch in developing those traits. The ranch "is a big, isolated, tough, hard outfit located in a hostile desert environment subject to all of the forces of nature such as drought, winds, floods, grasshoppers, range fires, predators, and almost anything else you want to mention," an Arizona colleague of Sandra Day said. People who grow up in such an environment sometimes have an added dimension of character, and he thinks Sandra has it to a high degree.

Her brother Alan Day put it succinctly: "This dried-up old piece of desert is what we are."

But at age sixteen, in the summer of 1946, Sandra Day was a young woman ready for the intellectual stimulation of a large university. She was trying on new clothes that summer, ready to launch herself in the world. American society at that time was telling young women to stay home and let returning GIs have their jobs back. There is no indication that Sandra paid much attention to the stay-at-home advice.

# 3

# Becoming a Lawyer

Sandra Day blossomed during her first year at Stanford. The university was not only a much larger world than the ranch, Lordsburg, or El Paso. It was filled with peers more nearly her equal in intelligence and seriousness of purpose. By the end of six years there, she had amassed an outstanding academic record, met her husband and another future Supreme Court justice, and impressed everyone with her quiet determination to make good.

Stanford University in the late 1940s and early 1950s provided an Ivy League–type education on the West Coast. It attracted the sons and daughters of the wealthy and a flood of World War II veterans ready to make up for lost time. Founded by Leland Stanford in 1891, the university had a campus of 1,500 acres near Palo Alto, California, when Sandra arrived.

At first she was reserved with the other

freshman women at Branner Hall, but she soon got to know them during meals, dorm social functions, and late-night conversations. Men outnumbered women, five to two, and women were more restricted socially. House mothers stood at the door each weeknight at ten o'clock to check the women students into the dorms.

Sandra hardly needed the imposed discipline. She was so excited by the vast array of liberal arts courses that were required or offered her first year that she found it hard to settle on a major. At a time when many women chose education, she considered geology and "even English" but settled on economics.

One of her sophomore roommates, Marilyn Schwartz, was also an economics major. The two did pages and pages of cost accounting together. Marilyn recalls that despite being part of a small minority of women in economics, Sandra was never afraid to speak up in class.

Once into economics, Sandra completed the tough sequence in three years. No only did she work hard, get everything done, and make fabulous grades but she went into her subjects "much more thoroughly than some of the rest of us," Marilyn said, and was ready to discuss them with her professors.

Of all the courses Sandra took as an undergraduate, she remembers particularly the class in business law taught by Professor Harry John Rathbun. The course was actually an introduction to legal thinking, as Professor Rathbun was a member of the law school faculty. The course often convinced students to go to law school or persuaded them not to. For Sandra it had the former effect.

Professor Rathbun and his wife Emilia also taught a seminar in their home, a critical study of the teachings of Jesus. Using a book by Henry Burton Sharman called *Jesus as Teacher*, the seminar was based on the premise that Jesus was one of the great teachers; it did not hinge on a particularly Christian point of view. This rather radical approach to religious ideas appealed to critically minded students like Sandra.

College was never all study. Sandra was known for her great sense of humor and the twinkle in her eyes. She enjoyed doing things with people, whether going out to a drive-in to escape the dorm food or attending dances and movies. There were skiing weekends at Yosemite and vacations at the homes of new friends in California and Oregon.

When it was her turn to entertain friends, Sandra invited them home to the ranch for round-up. Roundups occur twice a year. The cattle that roam year round over the thousands of acres are rounded up in several areas for counting and sorting—some to go to market, some to be sold for breeding, others to roam longer. Roundups begin each day before daybreak, when the riders saddle up, and last until dusk. Each rider's job is to round up the cattle and drive them toward the sorting area for the day.

When Sandra appeared at the Lazy B with two Stanford classmates—Beatsie (Beatrice) Challis and Calista Farrell—Harry complained that he didn't have time to play wet nurse to three dude girls. They would have to saddle their own, he said. So they did, and proved themselves adequate cowgirls.

In many ways Sandra was leading a privileged life. She did not have to hold down a job to help pay for her education, though extra hands were always welcome at the ranch. The Days were not wealthy, but they were able to send Sandra to a private school for many years, to pay for a college education, and to travel. Household help was present in the homes she lived in from time to time. That didn't mean Sandra didn't work hard herself, but it did free her to focus her efforts on the things she considered important.

She considered her studies very important. After meeting all the academic challenges in sight on the undergraduate level, she began thinking about life after college. The business law course had introduced her to the intellectual possibilities of law. Stanford had just started a 3-3 program whereby students could start their first year of law school while finishing their fourth year of college.

Sandra had never really planned to become a lawyer, but she began thinking about the program. Fewer than 3 percent of law students at that time were women, and some of the law schools, including Harvard, did not even admit women. As usual, there is no indication she paid any attention to the odds. Her parents had always supported her ambitions—her father liked the prospect of having a lawyer in the family—and her friends encouraged her, too, knowing she could do it.

So she applied—and was accepted. Applying for what she wanted and winning by merit was becoming a pattern in her life. She was awarded her B.A. from Stanford the following spring, magna cum laude—with great distinction—after she had already completed the first year of law school.

The first year of law school is known as the test of a student's mettle, more so when Sandra was going to law school than now. One-third of a class usually flunked out the first year, so fear of being "rolled out" was high. Three years younger than most of her classmates, Sandra dug in. The first year was tough but marvelous, she recalls, because "there were so many things to study at once." She was not the type to panic, but she did make sure she was well prepared for each class.

During the first week of school, Sandra found an ally—Beatrice Challis, who had graduated from the University of California in political science. The class of 150 first-year students had been divided into two sections at about the letter K in the alphabet, to fit into the old law school classrooms. Sandra and Beatsie were the only two women in the A–K half; there were five in the other section.

"I was dying to meet her" that first week, Beatsie remembers. "I kept looking over at her." Sandra had naturally curly hair, quite short and dark. She wore skirts and sweaters and usually hose and flat heels and had a distinctive style that suited her, unlike Beatsie's California coed look—socks and saddle or buckskin shoes, baggy sweaters with round collars. Once the two met, they sat next to each other in class and conferred often.

By March and April of the first year, tension among the law students was high. Except for one exam in torts, all the exams were held in June, and students had little concrete evidence of how they were doing until then. Beatsie and Sandra joined a small study group to go over sample test questions and take cases apart.

The atmosphere of the law school was impersonal and competitive. Enrollment had more than doubled after the war. In Sandra's second year there were four hundred law students, with fewer than ten women. Professors, as a result, made less of an attempt to get to know each student, although they made themselves available to those who wanted to get to know them.

In class they used the Socratic method of questioning students about the cases they had read. The method was designed to teach students to be well prepared and to think on their feet. Professors could be harsh in their questioning and sarcastic in their responses to students' answers. A student's performance in class and on final exams had a great deal to do with finding a good job after graduation.

Some alumnae remember no distinctions being made between men and women in class. Often the professors were still rather courtly. Other women recall being picked on by professors. At a time when not all women graduates actually became lawyers, women were often resented for "taking a man's place" in the class.

Sandra seemed to have been unaffected by any sex-based distinctions. She did well on her exams, and academic achievements made her an unquestioned equal. Classmates remember her as brilliant, and professors as very determined to make good.

One measure of her success was that she became an editor of the *Stanford Law Review* and a member of Order of the Coif. Being an editor of a school's law review is considered an honor. Editors select, edit, and check articles they want to publish in a quarterly review. Order of the Coif is a national honorary group that accepts only the best law students.

The people she met at law school were also important. Classmates would become valuable professional contacts later. Besides her husband, she met and became good friends with William Rehnquist, who was appointed to the Supreme Court in 1972. Rehnquist was a returning veteran who was dating Sandra's housemate, Calista. Sandra crammed for first-year final exams with him. Thirty years later her chambers at the Supreme Court would be next to his.

Friendships then were the beginning of what has been called the old boys' network. The term describes a group of men who attended college and graduate school together and then went into careers where their paths continued to cross. They can be very helpful to one another with news of jobs opening up, recommendations for promotion, and so forth.

Despite her sex, Sandra was becoming accepted by the Stanford old boys' network because she had gone to Stanford and done well. Later, as a member of the alumni board and then as a trustee, she met other politically influential Stanford graduates living in different sections of the country. Several went to bat for her when she was first considered for the Supreme Court.

Her closest friends, however, were the women at Cubberley House, where Sandra lived during her last two years in law school. Cubberley House was a large wooden house at the top of a hill, Santa Ynez. From the big front porch one looked down at the row of fraternity and sorority houses leading away from Stanford. Inside the house were mahogany paneling, comfortable Morris chairs, and lots of wicker, which gave the place a 1910 aura. Across the back fence and hidden from Stanford's view by Cubberley House was the president's house. (When Mrs. Cubberley died, her house was torn down to open up the view.)

The house belonged to the widow of Dr. Ellwood P. Cubberley, a longtime dean of the School of Education. After he died, Mrs. Cubberley (Helen van Uxem) decided to invite graduate women to live in their house.

Cubberley House was run as a cooperative, with each of the eleven women taking turns cooking the evening meal. Beatsie had chosen Stanford Law School over Berkeley and Yale mainly because of the warmth and female companionship of

Cubberley House. She invited Sandra there for dinner the first year when Sandra was still living in Union Residence. Sandra moved in the second year and became close friends with Calista Farrell, who was in the Graduate School of Education, Beatsie, and Catherine (Kitty) Lockridge, who was in the class of 1952 at the law school. Mrs. Cubberley kept the front parlor for her own use and shared the other rooms with women graduate students of physics and English as well as education and law.

Law students were frequent visitors at the house for dinner, parties, or study sessions. Sandra always had time for fun. "She was a terribly well organized person, but you never saw her organizing," Calista said. "We knew she studied, but you were never aware of it." She must have been a hard person to keep up with—never in a flap or a rush, always making time to do what she wanted.

During her Stanford years Sandra dated various men, one seriously enough to wear his ring on a chain around her neck. But for unrecollected reasons she had a "horrendous" breakup with the young man. Soon thereafter, in the spring of 1952, a new young man began appearing regularly at Cubberley House; he was John J. O'Connor III.

John O'Connor was the son of a prominent San Francisco doctor. His father's father had immigrated from Ireland and settled in San Francisco, where he was administrator of St. Francis Hospital during the earthquake of 1906. John was two months older than Sandra but a year behind her in law school. The story of how they met has become a local legend.

Both were editors of the *Stanford Law Review*, a prestigious but demanding job. One part of an editor's task was to check all of an article's citations to cases to make sure that the case or decision is correctly cited and that the decision says what the article writer claims it says. Many articles have more than a hundred citations, so "cite-checking" is not a frivolous task.

John and Sandra had been assigned to cite-check such an article together one January evening in 1952. "We did the cite-checking in the library," John remembers, "and I suggested we do the proofreading over a beer." They managed to turn that into so much fun that they spent the next forty-six evenings together before agreeing to spend an evening apart.

"I remember her coming back and saying she had met somebody who was really fun," Beatsie relates. "I thought he must be fun if it was fun to cite-check together."

A wedding date was eventually set for December 20, 1952, at the ranch. Her father's reaction? "We liked John, but I've seen better cowboys."

What Sandra found in John was a sense of humor that matched her own, an ability to spin a good story, a good dancer, a supportive husband, and eventually a fine and prosperous lawyer. They were a strong pair, matched in intelligence and interests. Neither would dominate the other. Because they went into different kinds of law, they never competed directly with each other.

After graduation that spring, Sandra had interviews with law firms in Los Angeles and San Francisco. Because she was an editor of the *Law Review* and in the top 10 percent of her class, she might have expected to be among the most sought-after graduates that year. But in 1952 none of those private law firms had ever hired a woman.

Women lawyers were "a bizzare thing" then, said Shirley Hufstedler, secretary of education in the Carter administration, who had graduated from Stanford three years before Sandra. Only about 4 percent of lawyers were women. The only law firms that offered them jobs were those owned by a father, brother, or husband.

For the first time in her life, Sandra found that merit did not work for her. Every law firm she applied to turned her down. Many declined even to interview her. They were just "not interested in hiring a woman," a phrase that was to recur in her life. One firm did offer her a job—as a legal secretary—provided she could type well.* To her everlasting credit, she turned it down.

Sandra did not appear terribly disappointed by the rejections. "I think Sandra was shooting for the top" when she applied for those jobs, Calista said. "I don't think she really expected to get it. We just accepted it then: it was the tenor of the times. We expected it would be tough" for women.

*That firm—Gibson, Dunn, and Crutcher of Los Angeles—was the firm of William French Smith, the attorney general who later helped select O'Connor for the Supreme Court.

In fact Sandra was very pleased when she was offered a job as a law clerk with the San Mateo County district attorney. (She was later promoted to deputy district attorney.) The job would allow her to work and still be close to John, who was finishing his third year of law school. Finding a government job was the usual alternative for women lawyers. The public sector was more open to women than private firms were. Sandra would say later that being redirected into public service turned out to be very beneficial.

That didn't mean she would stop shooting for the top, however. What struck those who knew her then was her determination, a quiet determination that you seldom saw but that ran strong and deep and would keep her on course through the next twelve years of juggling family and career.

The wedding the following December was a bit unusual. It might have been held in San Francisco, close to Stanford friends and John's family, but Sandra wanted it at the ranch. The ceremony took place in front of the fireplace in the very crowded living room of the Days' home. It was led by an Episcopalian minister (although John was a Catholic) and wire-recorded, an old recording process using magnetic wire.

The reception was held in the barn, a brand-new barn with a corrugated roof and rafters decorated with pine boughs gathered from the mountains. Guests sat on hay bales or danced to the music of a local band and ate Lazy B barbecued beef. The cowboys wore neckties and waltzed Stanford graduates around the floor, their arms pumping like crazy.

While many of the guests bedded down at the ranch, Sandra and John drove to El Paso, then went on to Mexico City by plane and a honeymoon in Acapulco. After Christmas it was back to law.

Despite the job setback, everything was coming together for Sandra. To a strong family and educational background she had added outstanding academic achievements, excellent career preparation, and a personal base for happiness. The rest of her life she would build on these foundations, until she did in fact reach the top.

# 4

# Family First

After a strong start in college and law school, Sandra O'Connor spent the next twelve years as many young adults do: trying out different jobs, making decisions about where to live and about having children, developing friendships, and putting down roots in a community. During her twenties and early thirties, Sandra was a wife, mother, lawyer, and community volunteer, and somehow she managed to do all of those jobs well.

Before the whirlwind began, she and John had five years together without major responsibilities. John's only obligation was his military one. When he graduated from Stanford in 1953, he expected to be drafted. He spent the summer in San Francisco, working on a book with trial lawyer Melvin Belli. Then he entered the army in October as a private.

He didn't remain a buck private for long. On an

exciting day in his life, John was commissioned a second lieutenant and ordered to Charlottesville, Virginia, to train in the Judge Advocate General's Corps, the lawyers' unit of the army. He was to be stationed in West Germany, so Sandra applied for a job with the army, too—and got it.

In her first two jobs, Lawyer Day O'Connor was just getting her feet wet. In the district attorney's office she did legal research on civil cases. She wrote legal opinions concerning the powers and duties of various public officers. After leaving the district attorney's office to join John, who was then in the army, she worked as a civilian lawyer for the Quartermaster's Corps for three years, from 1954 to 1957, in Frankfurt am Main.

Her job in the Quartermaster's Corps was to read the fine print in contracts. The quartermaster buys food and supplies for the army and also disposes of surplus equipment. Sandra was to review the contracts and handle any disputes that arose from them.

As always, there was time for fun. During their three years in Germany, the O'Connors toured some fourteen European countries. When John's tour of duty came to an end in December 1956, they decided to stay on through the winter and ski. They rented a cottage in the Austrian Alps, in the town of Kitzbühel, and—to be safe—they bought their tickets home.

Then they skied every day for three months. Sandra mused with a smile that she thought she would get tired of skiing, "but I didn't." When the snow melted in the spring and their money ran out, the five years of mere couplehood were almost over. Sandra was pregnant, and they decided to go home.

Home was to be Phoenix. The couple had considered California where John had family, both had friends, and both had been admitted to the bar. But Sandra's Arizona roots were strong. The O'Connors decided they wanted an urban setting where they could be active in community affairs. The state capital seemed the best place to do that, so they chose Phoenix.

It turned out to be a wise choice. Since air conditioning had made the summers bearable, Phoenix was undergoing explosive growth. Large numbers of talented, educated, and moneyed people were moving to Arizona. Many were people like Sandra who had strong ties to agriculture and ranching but wanted to live in the city. When the O'Connors left Phoenix twenty-four years later, Sandra described Arizona as "a land of opportunity and happiness."

The first task, however, was to pass the Arizona bar exam. (Each state licenses lawyers and requires them to pass a bar exam, demonstrating their knowledge of the state's law.) The only bar review course was in Tucson, so the O'Connors rented an apartment and spent the summer of 1957 taking classes in the morning, discussing cases around the swimming pool in the afternoon, and going back for more classes at night. Sharing the swimming pool and the discussions was a University of Michigan and Princeton graduate, Tom Tobin. Tobin was also thinking of making Arizona his home.

All three passed the exam. On October 5, nine

months pregnant, Sandra was sworn in before a judge of the Arizona state courts. Three days later, Scott Hampton O'Connor was born. Sandra wasn't sure at the time that she would make the swearing-in, but as usual her timing was excellent.

During the next few years the O'Connors began establishing themselves in the community. That fall John joined the law firm of Fennemore, Craig, von Ammon and Udall in downtown Phoenix. They bought an acre and a half of land in north Phoenix, and soon they began making plans to build a house.

Early on, the O'Connors were an upcoming young couple to watch. Phoenix's newspaper, the *Arizona Republic*, reported the unusual feat when they passed the bar together and when John joined Fennemore. It photographed John and Sandra for a feature article on babies and sex-role identification when Scott was less than a month old. And the newspapers noted when John was elected president of the Maricopa County Young Republicans Club in 1960.

While John was starting as an associate at Fennemore, Sandra was home taking care of Scott. But soon that was not enough. When Tom Tobin returned from six months overseas, the O'Connors invited him for dinner at their apartment, and he discussed his plans for starting out in the law in Phoenix. He wanted to work with an older lawyer on a new community development north of Scottsdale, but he also wanted to start a neighborhood law practice on the other side of Phoenix, in Maryvale.

Sandra learned to ride a horse at an early age on the Lazy B Ranch. Her favorites were Chico and Flaxey. She posed on Flaxey at age eight. (Photo: Harry and Ada Mae Day)

Some of Sandra's friends from the Radford School joined her at the ranch during Easter vacation in 1940. Sandra is second from the left. The toddler is her sister Ann. (Photo: Harry and Ada Mae Day)

Sandra's parents, Harry A. and Ada Mae Day, still live on the ranch where she grew up.

The Lazy B spreads over thousands of acres of semi-desert land on the Arizona-New Mexico border, an environment that taught Sandra self-reliance.

At age sixteen Sandra was an accomplished graduate of El Paso's Austin High School (this picture is from the yearbook), ready to take on Stanford. (Photo: Harry and Ada Mae Day)

Sandra Day takes a respite from law school. Skiing weekends were a welcome diversion from the books. (Photo: Harry and Ada Mae Day)

Mrs. Day greets John and Sandra on her visit to Germany during the O'Connors' three-year stint with the U.S. Army. (Photo: Harry and Ada Mae Day)

Sandra saw an opportunity. "If you want to be in Scottsdale part of the time, I could cover the west side office for you," she offered. Thus Tobin & O'Connor was launched in the spring of 1958. It was a neighborhood practice in a small office development in Maryvale, an area where many newcomers to Phoenix lived.

The arrangement was ideal for Sandra. She hired a baby-sitter in the mornings so that she could work till 1:00 or 2:00 P.M. Tom spent his mornings in Scottsdale and came to the Maryvale office in the afternoon. That gave Sandra time to spend with Scott and drop off John's reserve uniforms at the laundry. It was not the kind of arrangement she could have negotiated with a downtown Phoenix firm.

Tobin & O'Connor handled a variety of cases. Walk-in clients wanted advice on house purchases, landlord-tenant obligations, drunken driving tickets, and collecting damages for injuries from automobile accidents. The two young lawyers also signed up to defend indigents, people who had been accused of a crime but who couldn't afford a lawyer. The court would assign them lawyers from the list of those willing and pay the lawyers a small fee. The defendant gained a lawyer, and the lawyer gained experience in trials, plea bargaining, and the sentencing procedure. Sandra began to experience the difference between the law school classroom and the courtroom.

With a second child on the way in late 1959, Sandra told Tom that Maryvale was too far to drive and that she would have to give up her part of the practice. Subsequently, Tobin & O'Connor became Tobin & Tupper for a while, and Sandra returned to full-time mothering for five years.

She worked hard at being a good mother. Brian was born in January 1960, followed by Jay in May 1962. Sandra recalls the at-home years as a busy time when she was juggling a lot of things, "more than at any period of my life."

Her sister Ann moved to Phoenix in 1964, and the two became quite close while raising their families. They sent their children to the same camps and registered them for swimming and tennis lessons. The O'Connor boys went either to a private school—Phoenix Country Day, which was only half a block away—or to public school, whichever seemed right for each son. For high school, they went to Brophy, a structured, Jesuit-run school.

Scott, Brian, and Jay all demonstrated athletic ability, as did their mother. They spent many hours over the years at the Paradise Valley Country Club, where Sandra played golf and tennis. The family eventually developed a tradition of skiing "on the steepest hill we can find" on Christmas Day.

Summers the boys often spent time on the Day ranch, where foreman Cole Webb taught them to ride and rope. The O'Connors told Jay that if anything ever happened to them, he could live on the ranch. Jay saved up the ten-dollar bus fare to the ranch, just in case.

Sandra's immersion in domestic life was not at all unusual for the early 1960s. Although Betty

Friedan was writing *The Feminine Mystique*, about being stifled in the suburbs, the women's movement was still a decade away. So between diapers, play groups, car pools, and swimming lessons, Sandra worked out her priorities. Her first priority was her family.

Her commitment to the family was not just a personal feeling. She saw the family as important to the foundation of society. When she became a judge she gave the following message to the couples she married: "Marriage is far more than an exchange of vows. It is the foundation of the family, mankind's basic unit of society, the hope of the world, and the strength of our country. It is the relationship between ourselves and the generations which follow."

From the time the O'Connors returned to Phoenix from Germany, they had been planning their family home. It was to be in Paradise Valley, in north Phoenix. Paradise Valley was developing where unreclaimed desert land had existed in the 1940s, in the shadow of Camelback Mountain. The area, where Senator Barry Goldwater also built a home, eventually became known as a millionaires' ghetto.

The O'Connors started out modestly. When their house was near completion, both pitched in to soak the adobe bricks in coat after coat of skimmed milk before they were baked, an old technique. The house grew as the boys grew; a swimming pool and guest house were added in 1972.

As Phoenix grew, the house turned out to be a

prime investment. When it went on the market in 1982, the asking price was $350,000. John's share in his law firm was also growing. When he started in 1957, he was earning about $300 a month. When he left, he was a partner with a $342,850 interest in the firm. Besides owning a share of the Lazy B, the O'Connors invested in stocks and real estate ventures.

Obviously, John was a very successful lawyer. His firm also profited from the rapid economic growth Phoenix was undergoing. In the early 1960s, some 2,500 new people moved into the city or its nearer suburbs every month. An article in the *Saturday Evening Post* in 1961 described seven "New Millionaires of Phoenix," whose fierce ambition had made them money in building, manufacturing, or land speculation.

As a native daughter, Sandra was in a good position to become a leader of the professional class moving into north Phoenix. Her career in public service would benefit, too, from the expansion of government jobs as the private economy expanded.

Both O'Connors worked hard for their success. John was not one to pitch in and help with the diapers or dirty dishes. "I would be the last one to tell the boys to learn how to iron or cook," he told the *Ladies' Home Journal*. "I've never done either, and I don't expect to," not out of principle but because of incompetence. But he did support his wife in other ways. His income enabled her to hire household help. Freed from some of the domestic routine, she could look for ways to use her professional skills, which she soon did. Behind every successful woman lawyer, it has been said, stands a supportive husband and good household help. Sandra had both.

Thus, by virtue of their family background, education, income, and home in a prime neighborhood, the O'Connors were associating with people of the upper middle and upper classes. Both liked to socialize, and they invited people for dinner frequently. Sandra is known as an excellent cook and a gracious hostess and John as a spinner of anecdotes and tales. They made so many friends that in 1982, when they left Phoenix, 850 came to a farewell dinner.

But that's getting ahead of the story. In the early 1960s Sandra was still juggling three sons, cooking, volunteer activities, and Republican politics. How the O'Connors became pillars of their community could be a textbook example.

John was active in Republican politics, the Paradise Valley Zoning and Planning Commission, and the Maricopa County Hospital Advisory Board. Sandra volunteered or was drafted for nearly everything—from the YMCA to the Phoenix Historical Society. (She would later describe clubs as great training grounds for developing executive abilities.)

She joined the Republican party, too, at a time when Barry Goldwater was fashioning it into a strong alternative to Arizona's dominant rural Democrats. Newcomers to the state began to give the Republicans enough votes to wrest control away from the Democrats. Sandra became actively involved as a county precinct committee member from 1960 to 1964, legislative district chairman from 1962 to 1965, and acting vice-chairman of the Maricopa County Republican Committee in 1964. Senator Goldwater, whose Arizona brand of conservative Republicanism became known nationwide when he ran for President in 1964, was to become an important associate.

Along with political activism came appointments to various government commissions: the Maricopa Board of Adjustments and Appeals, the Governor's Commission on Marriage and the Family, and the Arizona State Personnel Commission. Eventually Sandra had joined or been appointed to all of the "right" boards, committees, and political groups in Phoenix, according to the Phoenix newspaper.

Despite her heavy involvement in civic activities, Sandra could be sensitive to the needs of individuals. When a cowboy from the ranch, one she hadn't known, came to Phoenix sick and epileptic, she looked after him and helped him find a job when he recovered. Similarly, she was sympathetic when an unmarried young woman who helped with her housekeeping became pregnant. She continued to employ her until the baby was due.

Finally, Sandra was involved in so many different activities that she thought a paid job would make her life more orderly. Jay was three, old enough for preschool; Brian was five, and Scott was eight. Sandra, at age thirty-five, thought the time was right for resuming her career. Planning to manage both family and job was just another challenge to her organizing skills.

William Eubank, then chief assistant to the attorney general of Arizona, recalls a phone call he received one day from Sandra O'Connor. She said she had a problem. Her husband was working for a large law firm, and her children were still small. She was looking for a part-time job, because she wanted to be able to take her children to school and pick them up afterward.

Her desire to work but still be home when her children were there struck a responsive chord in Eubank. Sandra remembers that it was hard to get the job, that "they weren't very interested in hiring a woman." The attorney general's office was small, with about twenty attorneys, and turnover was low. When an opening occurred, those who had applied most recently were most likely to be hired. O'Connor persisted and eventually reached Eubank at an opportune time. He had "half a salary" sitting around unused, so he hired her.

It may have been a modest start, but, once started, O'Connor's career never slowed down. Her job as an assistant attorney general was to represent state agencies like the Arizona State Hospital (for the mentally ill) and the Arizona Children's Hospital. She represented them in court, advised them on how state laws applied to them, and lobbied for them in the legislature.

She would appear in the office at about 10:00 A.M., work through till 2:30, and rush home, often taking work with her. If she had to be in court before 10:00 or after 2:30, she would make the necessary arrangements for her children. Soon she was asking for more work, something more challenging that would involve going to court more often. Her legal opinions were so good that other lawyers soon sought her advice.

"She obviously was brilliant, knew what she was doing," said Gary Nelson, one of the attorneys general she worked for. "You always liked to get her opinion about things, even if it wasn't in her area." Eventually, as her sons got older, she began to work full-time and handle some of the tougher cases in the office. One colleague felt that she was destined for "more than a windowless office in the attorney general's office."

Just as she had turned to working for the government when private firms turned her down, Sanda followed another route common to women when she took a part-time job that allowed her to meet her family responsibilities. Once she proved herself indispensable, the job became full-time. A good friend pointed out that O'Connor "understands very well the conflict between a woman's desire to be part of the professional world and yet to be a perfect mother and wife as well."

As she began working again in 1965, the women's movement was awakening. The Report of the President's Commission on the Status of Women and Betty Friedan's *The Feminine Mystique* had both been released in 1963. That same year an Equal Pay Act passed Congress, followed by the Civil Rights Act of 1964, which prohibited discrimination on the basis of sex as well as race. (The addition of sex had been proposed as a joke by eighty-one-year-old Virginia Congressman Howard W. Smith.) In 1966 the National Organization for Women (NOW) was established.

Though never active in the women's movement, Sandra was blazing ahead in her own calling—the law. Other women in Arizona were doing the same. Margaret Hance was the first woman mayor of a large city (Phoenix). Sandra semed almost to be following in the footsteps of Lorna Lockwood. Lockwood, a Democrat, had been an assistant attorney general. She served in the legislature, was a judge on the Maricopa County Superior Court, and was, from 1965 to 1975, the first woman chief justice of a state supreme court. The career pattern had been outlined.

Sandra was about to take the next step. As she worked in the attorney general's office, she became quite familiar with state government. Her legal opinions were quoted in the newspaper in articles about state government issues, and she earned a reputation for being top-notch, hardworking, fair, and correct. She also remained extremely active in Republican politics. The Republicans had taken over the Arizona state legislature in 1966 and had elected a Republican governor, John R. Williams.

Three years later Sandra was rewarded for her years of party work toward that victory. Isabella Burgess, the state senator from O'Connor's legislative district, was resigning to take a job in Washington with the National Transportation Safety

Board. Sandra was asked if she was interested in the vacancy. She definitely was. Once she had made up her mind to be a state senator, she applied to the Maricopa County Board of Supervisors and was appointed.

# 5

# Excelling in Politics

Sandra O'Connor came into Arizona's legislature at a prime time for Republicans. The party had won a majority in both houses in 1966, for the first time in the state's history. Most of the new Republicans represented the cities of Phoenix and Tucson, whose growing populations had come to represent 80 percent of the state's people. The courts forced a reapportionment that gave Maricopa County (mainly Phoenix) thirteen new seats in the state senate. Sandra occupied one of them. Although she came from a remote area of the state, she was very much a metropolitan person.

Having been a minority for so long, in a rural and Democratic-controlled legislature, the Republicans were eager to make some changes in the way Arizona was governed. In two years they had passed a strong anti-smog law, revamped a scandal-ridden Liquor Control Board, written a new ethics law, and tackled uniform property-evaluation and assessment. During O'Connor's first three years, they added a no-fault divorce statute, a flood control act, and a total reorganization of state government.

As usual, Senator O'Connor quickly demonstrated her capability. She earned a reputation for being a perfectionist in drafting bills and for always being prepared with the facts when she spoke up in the Senate. She was extremely hardworking. "During the time the legislature is in session, I devote my whole life to it," she explained to a reporter. "I have to write off everything else, I'm afraid."

As one of the two women senators, she was something of a curiosity. The author of an article in *Phoenix* magazine in 1971 described her as "Arizona's beauteous senator . . . a lively, lissome creature" who drew "appreciative but sub-sonic" wolf whistles from her colleagues. Her response to such attention was straightforward. She expected to be evaluated on the basis of her accomplishments, not her looks. Indeed, the article speculated that she had contributed more key legislation her first year than "any fledgling legislator in Arizona's history."

Her appearance also conveyed the message of serious intent. She dressed simply, formally, and well. Her hairstyle was simple, too, wavy and moderate in length. She admitted to having two advantages: she did not have to support her family on a legislator's $6,000 salary, and she did not have to take time away from another job (besides her family) to be in the Senate. Her husband's salary and their prudent investments allowed her the economic freedom to be in public service.

One colleague recounted the successive impressions she made: "When you first meet Sandra you think, 'What a pretty little thing.' Next you think, 'My, it's got a personality, too.' After listening a bit you begin to wonder how that quietly feminine voice can pack so much fact power. From then on, it's but a step to discovery that this pretty little thing carries a disconcerting load of expertise."

Because she represented a fairly safe district— it was five to one Republican—Sandra had the luxury of voting in the way she thought was right. She did not feel she had to follow the swings of public sentiment. When first appointed, Senator O'Connor described herself as "a fiscal conservative and a moderate Republican." She believed that all laws should treat all people fairly, that the cost of government should remain reasonable, and that the actions of government should be a matter of public knowledge.

Many of the issues she supported were "good government" laws: making meetings of government bodies open to the public, coordinating services for the mentally retarded, and selecting judges for the Superior Court on the basis of merit. She was good, too, at writing complicated bills like the one that equalized the finances of rich and poor counties.

On some issues she was definitely conservative. She opposed gun control, supported a resolution calling on Congress to end forced busing for integration, and voted to reinstate the death penalty in Arizona. She was described as a liberal in her support of a family planning bill and for guaranteeing reporters the right to protect their confidential sources.

But the best word to describe her was independent. She would study the law carefully, look at the pros and cons of an issue, and make up her own mind. The bills she supported gave ample evidence of her independent views. She led a complete revision of Arizona's mental health laws, providing periodic reviews for people in mental institutions. She favored bilingual education for Arizona's large Spanish-speaking population and workers' compensation for migrant farm workers. She supported Medicaid and provisions in the anti-pollution law that forced the copper companies to eliminate noxious sulphur dioxide from smelters. She was almost the only senator willing to oppose publicly state aid to private schools, even though she served on the board of the private Phoenix Country Day School.

Early in her legislative career, she was an enthusiastic leader on women's issues. She was the first Arizona legislator to introduce the Equal Rights Amendment for ratification after ERA had passed Congress on March 22, 1972. She wanted Arizona to be the first state to ratify ERA, but Hawaii acted the same day the amendment passed Congress. On March 24 she rose from her senate seat to urge her colleagues to pick up their dawdling pace and approve the ERA because it "stands in the tradition of other great amendments to the U.S. Constitution."

But the enthusiasm of the moment faded. Arizona's two U.S. senators, Barry Goldwater and Paul Fannin, were firmly opposed to the ERA. "She favored issues we could win," said a women's rights advocate, "and she began to think the ERA was a lost cause." She continued to support it, but the ERA never passed the Arizona legislature.

Senator O'Connor thought there were other ways to secure women's rights. She thought that cases already in the federal courts would solve some of the questions of equal pay and hiring practices. Meanwhile, some of the most discriminatory laws were state, not federal, laws. She set about making some practical changes for women in Arizona.

One change she helped to bring about was the repeal of the 1913 law that "protected" women from working more than eight hours a day. O'Connor said that instead of protecting them "it hinders them" from earning more money to support themselves and their families. Why, even the legislature was ignoring that law. Despite considerable opposition, the repeal bill passed the senate by one vote during her first two months. In another matter close to her own background, she helped to make girls as well as boys eligible for farm youth loans.

O'Connor maneuvered some changes in the state's community property laws, too—the laws that govern how money and property are to be shared and managed by a married couple. Her revision deleted some of the preferences given to men and husbands and inserted the woman's right to sign a contract binding on the couple. Alice Bendheim, whose law review article had urged a change, said O'Connor shepherded the changes through in a very shrewd way by making them part of a noncontroversial bill. In the process she had to smooth some ruffled feathers. "She's very, very efficient in that way, and she got it through."

Later in her career a great deal of scrutiny would be given to O'Connor's votes on abortion. During her first year in the state senate she voted in the Judiciary Committee to repeal Arizona's law prohibiting abortions. Under the law at that time, helping in an abortion was a felony punishable by two to five years in prison. O'Connor said she believed a change was appropriate.

In 1973 she cosigned a family planning bill that would have made birth control methods and information available to anyone who requested it. "It seemed to me that perhaps the best way to avoid having people who were seeking abortions," she explained, "was to enable people not to become pregnant unwittingly or without the intention of doing so." The bill was denounced by the *Arizona Republic*, Phoenix's leading newspaper, and it died in committee. In 1974 she voted against a "right-to-life memorial" that called on Congress to pass a constitutional amendment allowing the states to ban abortion.

Because she was a woman in the public eye,

Senator O'Connor was a frequent speaker to women's and student groups. A consistent theme in her speeches was the importance of the individual. The nature of society will always turn on the quality of the individual, she said. She urged individuals to become involved, to know the "vehicles of power in and out of government and how to influence them."

Her message to women echoed that of Margaret Mead: If women want real power and change, they must run for public office and use the vote more intelligently. She suggested to women that they persuade employers to provide part-time jobs and push for adequate day-care facilities and changes in the tax laws to allow the cost of child care as a deductible business expense.

O'Connor seemed to become less enthusiastic about women's issues the longer she stayed in the legislature. Certainly the political climate in Arizona did not favor the women's movement. Although she accomplished some of the changes feminists were urging, she did not approve of the most radical feminists because she thought they wanted to destroy the structure of society. In a campaign speech in the cafeteria of Camelback High School in 1970 she drew sustained laughter when she was asked about the women's movement. She replied in earnest: "I come to you tonight wearing my bra and my wedding band."

At the end of her first year in the legislature, Senator O'Connor was elected to the position to which she had earlier been appointed. At the end of the following two-year term she was reelected with the second highest number of votes among legislators. Her growing north Phoenix district had become the largest in the state.

Not only was she popular with her constituents but she had earned the respect of her colleagues, too. Shortly after the November 1972 elections, the eighteen Republican senators met at the San Marcos Hotel in Chandler, south of Phoenix. After a two-hour secret caucus, they emerged and reported that Sandra O'Connor had been selected as the new majority leader of the senate. No one seemed to notice then, but it was the first time in U.S. history that a woman had held that leadership position in a state legislature.

Sandra accepted that first in her matter-of-fact way: "I think my job as a legislative leader will be no different because I am a woman than it would be if I were a man," she said when the 1973 session began.

The job of the majority leader is to see that the bills proposed by the majority party (in this instance the Republican party) come to the floor of the senate for a vote and are passed. The job put her "in the middle of the action," where she liked to be. Sandra was "resolution-oriented," according to William Jacquin, the senate president who worked closely with her. Her approach was "Here's a problem; there has to be a resolution."

Sandra was not the kind of leader who twisted arms (that was William Jacquin's job). Her strength was in knowing the bills and their background inside and out. She didn't make a move until she had the facts and knew where she wanted to go with a bill. Then she was sensitive to arguments and opinions from all sides, but articulate enough to debate and point the way toward resolving the issue at the same time.

People who wanted to influence her or change her mind knew they had to be equally well prepared. "She worked interminable hours and read everything," said Democratic Senator Alfredo Guitierrez. "It was impossible to win a debate with her. We'd go on the floor with a few facts and let rhetoric do the rest. Not Sandy. She would overwhelm you with her knowledge."

The process of gaining agreement did not always go smoothly. O'Connor's forte was in preparing the bills to come to the floor. But she annoyed some of her fellow senators with what they called nit-picking—her attempts to correct what she saw as inaccuracies in their bills. (She was such a perfectionist that she once offered an amendment to a bill merely to insert a missing, but important, comma.) Once near the end of a session, a harried colleague said he'd like to punch her in the nose, but most admired her intelligence and preparation.

She looked feminine, but she had the toughness that comes from a disciplined mind. "She was as hard-nosed as they come in a floor fight, tougher in committee meetings, and absolutely ruthless in caucus, behind closed doors," said a frequent opponent.

To a reporter "she always looked as if she had something else to do. With her it was 'push or pull or get the hell out of the way.'"

One of her successes as majority leader was guiding though the legislature a state constitutional amendment that would limit the amount of money the state could spend. The idea was borrowed from California, where Ronald Reagan was governor. In Arizona, O'Connor proposed to limit state spending to 8.4 percent of the total personal income of the people in the state. The measure failed on the ballot in California, passed the legislature in Arizona, but failed on the ballot there, too. Not until 1980 did Arizona enact such a spending limit.

During the five years Sandra spent in the legislature, her sons were growing, the oldest entering high school. One of the advantages of being a legislator was that she had some months relatively free, when the legislature was not in session and she was not campaigning. She used her time to plan summer activities for the boys and elaborate family vacations, like rafting down Idaho's Salmon River.

When the legislature was in session, she had to use all her organizing abilities—thinking ahead, using every minute, shopping on the way home or at lunchtime. And sometimes—some few times—she couldn't do it all. She excused herself one night from a meeting of the legislature because "my boys are going to camp and I am going home to be sure they have packed everything."

Summers were the hardest times because the boys were out of school, and it was too hot for them to be outside. So she would look for active teenage boys—student body presidents or captains of football teams—to do things with the boys.

Her family returned her attention. When she turned forty in 1970, twenty-one long-stemmed roses were delivered to her office at the capitol. The card said, "You will always be twenty-one to us. The guys at 3651 East Denton Lane."

Being a legislator also gave her the opportunity to hone her matchmaking skills. She jokingly called herself "the yenta of Paradise Valley" because she introduced a number of couples, including her sister and brother-in-law. The key to her matchmaking was persistence. Ann Day Alexander relates how Sandra introduced her to her second husband, Scott Alexander.

"I was dating someone else at the time, teaching school in Phoenix. Scott, a state legislator, had been divorced for two years, and Sandra had been telling him she had a younger sister he should meet, but people had been telling him things like that too often. One afternoon Sandra called and said, 'I want you to be at my house for dinner tonight.' I said, 'I can't. I have a date,' but she was quite persuasive. We both came to dinner. Romance followed. She's quite good at sizing people up and seeing who would be a good match."

Sandra's five years in the legislature made her well-known to Arizonans. The legislature had traditionally been a strong governing body in the state, and those who succeeded there often went on to other political offices. There was speculation that O'Connor might be named a federal judge or state appeals court judge or that she might even run for governor. But none of these opportunities materialized immediately. She could also have run for the U.S. Congress, but that would have upended her family life.

During the legislative period Sandra had also perfected the skills that made her successful. The first was always being prepared. "I think that almost anything you do in life requires preparation," she says, "and if you are prepared and have thought about it, then things won't be a problem. If you are not prepared, that's grounds for concern."

From good preparation, self-confidence came. Asked how she developed the self-confidence she displays, she said that age does it best, that as you become older you pay less attention to what other people think of you; you rely more on yourself. She remembered being a self-conscious teenager like any other and being absolutely terrified the first time she had to speak in court. It took time to become comfortable in that kind of setting. She has learned, too, that people basically have a lot of goodwill.

It was also evident from the way she led her life that she set reasonable goals and worked toward them. After five years in politics, she had a new goal: to become a judge. She announced in April 1974 that she would not seek reelection to the senate, because she wanted to "get back into the mainstream of the law." (Others said the legislature was driving her crazy because of her own perfectionism.)

Several others in the Republican leadership

were leaving the legislature, too. Much had been accomplished, but it was time for new challenges. As Arizona continued to grow, so did the opportunities for public sector jobs. A new judgeship had been created, on the Maricopa County Superior Court, and Sandra decided to run for it.

# 6

# The Iron Judge

She stood in front of the judge asking for mercy. The thirty-seven-year-old mother of two babies—one three weeks old and the other sixteen months—had been convicted of writing bad checks totaling $3,500. She was facing a possible jail term of five to ten years, and she was begging the judge to give her probation so she could stay home with her children.

The judge, Sandra O'Connor, was herself the mother of three sons, but she believed deeply in the law and the system of government it upheld. She had been agonizing over the woman's fate for weeks. The woman was from a solid Scottsdale family and had been a successful, well-educated real-estate saleswoman. Why she had written bad checks, which may have actually totaled $100,000, was unknown. The woman had not committed a violent crime, but she had clearly broken the law.

Judge O'Connor finally decided that the woman should go to jail. Reporter Tom Fitzpatrick described the scene in an article in the _Arizona Republic_. "You have intelligence, beauty, and two small children," she said. "You come from a fine and respected family. Yet, what is depressing is that someone with all of your advantages should have known better."

When the judge announced the sentence of five to ten years in prison, the woman screamed. "What about my babies?" she wailed.

Judge O'Connor quickly left the courtroom and went to her chambers. She was found a few minutes later, crying at her desk. She says it was her hardest decision. (The woman spent eighteen months in jail and has since been reunited with her children.)

Sentencing people to prison was the most emotionally difficult part of being a judge. Day in and day out, Judge O'Connor saw human dramas unfolding in her courtroom. Her job was to run an orderly courtroom and ensure a fair trial, but when the verdict was in, she was the one who had to break the bad news of punishment to the defendant. O'Connor never shied away from making hard decisions. She was known from the beginning of her term as a tough judge who sent shivers through lawyers who appeared before her unprepared.

When she campaigned for the judgeship in 1974, crime was a big issue in Phoenix. The city ranked No. 1 in crime in the nation. O'Connor promised "as a citizen, a wife, and a mother" that she would "help replace fear in our streets with strength in our courtrooms." She won the primary (and subsequent general election) over David J. Perry, who had been appointed to the position less than three months before.

Sandra O'Connor spent five years as a trial judge in Maricopa County Superior Court, where trials are conducted for those charged with murder, rape, drug possession and sales, and burglary. The court also handles divorce and other civil cases. She sought the job because she wanted to return to law. At a time when executives in the government were going to trial for Watergate crimes, she believed that the system of justice worked. She called her job "administering old-fashioned justice in a modern age."

She administered justice with an iron hand. She ran a tight courtroom, where all the formalities were observed, dignity was maintained, and no nonsense was tolerated. She was very much the judge in her demeanor. "You have to say something awfully funny to get her to smile on the bench," one lawyer said.

Like her household, her courtroom ran smoothly, which meant she did not tolerate delay. If a lawyer asked for more time to prepare a case, she made him or her explain in open court why more time was needed. The explanations could be embarrassing. She took the legal process very seriously and was intolerant of anyone who took it lightly.

As a consequence, many lawyers were intimidated by her. "You didn't want to go in there if you weren't prepared, if you hadn't filed the papers when you were supposed to, if you hadn't researched your case properly, if you came in there on an argument without any authority and tried to snow her. . . . She did not appreciate having her time wasted," said lawyer Alice Bendheim.

On the other hand, if you were prepared and wanted a judge with an open mind, O'Connor's court was where you wanted to be. "If a lawyer was well prepared and all business, she was pretty easy to get along with," said former public defender John Foreman, who appeared before her many times. "Personally I like a judge like that. I found her to be fair, persuadable, and open-minded."

O'Connor's reputation as a judge who winks at nothing scared lawyers into being prepared, much as she had prompted other legislators to be prepared when they intended to debate her. Her own preparation for the day in court was extensive. She spent evenings reading for the next day's work and weekends and vacations reading to follow trends in the law.

She made some mistakes. In the trial of a woman convicted of hiring a hit man to kill a doctor for a share in a $24,000 deposit certificate, she made two wrong rulings on the prosecutor's conduct of the case. As a result, the Arizona Supreme Court overturned the conviction. "She had to rule quickly from the bench, and she blew it," the defense lawyer said. But, he added, "She's absolutely fair, and as an appellate judge, she'd have the chance and take the time to think through that decision, and I'd bet she'd overrule those rulings."

O'Connor was not afraid of making gutsy decisions. She sentenced one man to death after he had been convicted of murdering another man for a $3,300 fee, in a dispute over drugs. But when she found out that the prosecution had withheld important evidence from the defense lawyers she canceled that verdict and ordered a new trial.

In the murder-sodomy-arson trial of a man accused of burning his children to death in a trailer fire, she suppressed key evidence because the police had failed to obtain a search warrant at an important point in their investigation. Tom Henze, the defense lawyer, saw her ruling as an example of her devotion to the law. "I've seen her lean over the bench and look down and say, 'I don't like to do this, but this is what the law says,'" and then make a ruling like suppressing the important evidence.

Although she could be tough on defendants, she was sympathetic to a battered wife who had shot her husband. The jury found her guilty of murder, but O'Connor believed her plea of self-defense. She told the woman's lawyer she should not have been convicted and gave her the shortest jail term she could, by law. Then she wrote to the governor, supporting the woman's plea for mercy and a commutation (reduction) of her sentence.

In civil cases, she could be quite practical in forcing the litigants to solve their problems. Her husband relates the story of the greyhounds. Two lawyers in a divorce case were feuding about how to divide forty jointly owned greyhounds. The first witness went on for an hour with the life history of the first dog, in order to demonstrate its value. To avoid wasting the court's time, O'Connor called the two lawyers into her chambers. She told one of them to prepare two lists of dogs, the lists to be of equal value.

"When you finish," she said, "let the other attorney pick either one of the two lists for his client."

"In fifteen minutes," John J. O'Connor recalled in the *Washington Post*, "the litigation was over."

Especially in her first few years, O'Connor was a stiff sentencer. In addition to the jail term for the woman who wrote bad checks, she sentenced a murderer to death. She was especially hard on repeat offenders who had already been given a chance. Nor was she optimistic about rehabilitation. "We cannot impose the rehabilitative effect from the outside," she has said. "You can only make it possible for people to have the motivation so what they want to do is change their way of life." She believes the root cause of a high crime rate is a breakdown in the family unit.

As she gained experience, she began using her keen "people instinct" to become more flexible in sentencing. John Foreman cited a couple of cases that demonstrated her sensitivity to the differences in people. For example, she gave a minimum sentence to a bank robber Foreman represented "because she recognized his human qualities."

To a defendant convicted of eight sales of heroin and possession and sale of stolen property, O'Connor gave sixty days in a diagnostic center and then probation. "A lot of judges would not have had the courage to put that kid on probation," Foreman said. She took a chance on him, and it succeeded. He eventually earned a business degree and made a career in business.

After three years as a trial judge, O'Connor faced another career decision. She was asked in the spring of 1978 if she would run as a Republican candidate for governor. O'Connor had discussed the idea with other interested Republicans the previous fall, but none was able to muster enough support that early. As a judge, O'Connor could not really test the political waters openly by starting a campaign. In the spring she decided not to run. The Republican party in Arizona was disorganized and weakened by internal squabbling. Raising money would not be easy. For these and her own reasons she decided to remain a judge for the time being.

Democrat Bruce Babbitt was elected governor in November, and a year later he appointed Sandra to the state court of appeals. There were suggestions that Babbitt was trying to eliminate O'Connor as a possible opponent by putting her in a job she could not easily leave and return to. He insisted the selection was based on merit. "She had widespread respect within the judicial and law community," a press aide said. "She was just the kind of person the governor wanted to start off with. He wanted to start off on a high note."

In the late 1970s more opportunities were opening for women. O'Connor's election to a judgeship in 1974 had been facilitated by the fact that Arizona was growing fast and new judgeships were frequently created. In 1979, President Carter wanted to appoint women to the federal judiciary. He appointed Arizona apellate judge Mary Shroeder to the Ninth U.S. Circuit Court of Appeals, thus opening up the Arizona appellate position for O'Connor. O'Connor had a good education, ability, and experience, but she was also in the right place at the right time.

Being an appeals court judge was different from being a trial judge. Judges on the appeals court work together in panels of three to hear appeals from trials or hearings. They spend one day listening to lawyers argue why the original decisions were wrong or right and the rest of the week sitting at their desks reading or writing.

The appeals court in Arizona is in the new state capitol, a modern building with little of the carved wood and marble mustiness often associated with courts. One enters a plain reception area, with photographs of judges on the wall, a large room full of desks to the left, and a stark hall through doors to the right. Down that hall, behind doors with name plates, each of the nine judges has an outer office for the secretary and an inner, book-lined chamber for the judge. Sandra spent eighteen months there, researching, reading, and writing, relieved sometimes by lunches at a Mexican restaurant.

Sandra brought to the appeals court her precision, her thorough knowledge of the law, and her writing ability. She wrote thirty-two published opinions, in addition to memorandums that were not published.

The opinions gave the decision and reasoning of the judges who had heard the appeal. After listening to the lawyers' arguments, the three judges would discuss the case and see if they agreed on a decision. (If all three did not agree, the decision of two over one would prevail.) Then one of the three would be assigned to write the opinion.

The opinions O'Connor wrote were about fairly dull subjects, dull at least to those not affected by them. They concerned divorce settlements, bankruptcies, appeals from criminal convictions, landlord-tenant disputes, and industrial accidents. When she was nominated to the Supreme Court, O'Connor's opinions were read to find out how she might vote on constitutional issues, but the opinions gave few clues to her views on subjects like busing, school prayer, and free speech.

They did reveal her style of writing. The opinions were carefully reasoned, clear, "mercifully brief," and orderly. One description of her opinions was that they "tick off the law, tick off the precedents, and fit in the facts, all without rhetoric or asides."

When O'Connor was rated as a judge by lawyers in Arizona, she scored high on her attentiveness to arguments and her written opinions but lower on "courteousness to the litigants and lawyers" and on judicial temperament. Her impatience sometimes showed.

A few of her decisions were noteworthy. With the other judges on her panel, she ruled that a state law regarding tenants was discriminatory. The law said that if a landlord and tenant were arguing over the payment of the rent and the tenant was evicted, the tenant had to post twice the amount of a year's rent if he or she wanted to appeal the eviction. She said that was unfair to poor people, that the amount was too large. She also overturned the plea bargain and sentence of a rapist because he was under the influence of drugs when he confessed.

A more revealing source of her views was an article she wrote for the *William and Mary Law Review*. She had been invited to speak at a symposium on State Courts and Federalism in the 1980s at the law school in Williamsburg, Virginia, in January 1981. The article came from that talk. In it she urged more responsibility for the state courts and less intervention by the federal courts. She said state judges rivaled federal judges in competence and would protect the federal constitutional rights of defendants. "When the state court judge puts on his or her new federal court robe he or she does *not* become immediately better equipped intellectually to do the job," she wrote. She thought that access to the federal courts, especially in civil rights cases, should be more limited, at least until defendants had done all they could to air their complaints about due process or equal protection of the law in state courts.

While on the appeals court, Judge O'Connor

continued some of her volunteer work in the community at the leadership level. She was president of the Heard Museum, but she still waited in line for several hours like everyone else at the annual crafts sale. She was on the board of Blue Cross/Blue Shield and of the Phoenix Historical Society. In some of her posts she was able to keep in touch with the needs of those less fortunate than herself.

"I used to think she was totally cold," related a lawyer in the Maricopa County Public Defender's office, "until one day . . . she called me to say she'd heard from her work at the Salvation Army . . . of two people in jail who shouldn't be there, and whom we should petition the court to get released . . . She just had heard about it and thought we should do something. It's funny. She's supposed to be such a stiff, but she even told me that she had one of the wives of these people sitting in her office nursing a baby as we were speaking."

Sandra enjoyed the exchange of ideas with her fellow judges, whether over lunch or in discussions of an opinion she was drafting. She also reached out beyond Arizona's borders for intellectual and professional contacts. She had been selected as a trustee of Stanford in 1976; she met other distinguished graduates at the trustees' meetings. She organized a statewide women lawyers' association in 1980 and was a charter member of the National Association of Women Judges, started in 1979.

In the summer of 1980 she became acquainted with someone else who would be important in her future—Warren Burger, chief justice of the Supreme Court. They were both members of an Anglo-American legal exchange on criminal justice in London. Judge O'Connor recounted the trip to the other judges at the appeals court in bits and pieces over many luncheons. "Word had come back, much of it through Chief Justice Burger himself, that Judge O'Connor had made a tremendous impression on the English lords with her intricate knowledge of their procedures and her shrewd inquiries and observations," wrote Chief Judge Laurance T. Wren.

That October Ronald Reagan promised that, if elected, he would appoint a woman to the Supreme Court.

"Sandra, maybe you'll be it," a friend and politician told her.

"Well, thank you for thinking that of me," she replied, "but that would just never happen."

# 7

# A President's Promise

Judge O'Connor was working in her chambers late on a hot July afternoon when the phone rang in her secretary's office. It was no ordinary phone call.

The caller was none other than Chief Justice Warren Burger. Just as she began talking with him, another light flickered on the phone and she was interrupted by President Reagan, asking if she would accept his nomination to the Supreme Court. She remembers little of what he actually said, but she must have said yes. Within three months Judge O'Connor would become Justice O'Connor, and history was made.

Word spread quickly that afternoon at the court of appeals, and work in the usually staid surroundings came virtually to a halt. A deputy press secretary and secret service personnel flew in quickly from Washington as scores of reporters, photographers, and television camera operators began to converge on the scene. Sandra, who is not the type to let the cat out of the bag, told only her husband and sons. She called her sister Ann that evening and, without saying why, suggested she watch television the next morning. She couldn't reach her parents and brother on the ranch because their phone was out of order, a frequent occurrence in the remote area.

As Sandra prepared herself that evening, President Reagan prepared to make the announcement. On Tuesday morning, July 7, 1981, he told a large audience of reporters and photographers that he had found "a person for all seasons, a woman who meets the very high standards that I demand of all Court appointees." It was astounding news for her parents and brother when they saw it on television.

An hour and an half later, in Phoenix, O'Connor held her own press conference in her chambers. Looking very happy she said, "Good morning. This is a momentous day in my life and the life of my family." She answered a few questions as reporters began trying to find out about this relatively unknown woman. Then the congratulations poured in.

The announcement had "a tremendous impact on Division One of the Arizona Court of Appeals . . ." said Chief Judge Laurance T. Wren. "We were deluged by hundreds of phone calls from all over the United States. As one of our judges commented, it was as if we, too, had been vicariously appointed to the Court."

"I started to get on the phone to congratulate

my old friend [that morning]," said Phoenix Mayor Margaret Hance. "I found that to be absolutely impossible. You could not even dial the last number. After four hours I gave up trying, so I decided to send her a telegram. As I was dictating it to this young operator, my first words were, 'I am ecstatic,' and the young woman interrupted me and said, 'Oh, boy, so am I.'"

So many people were ecstatic because her nomination was the fulfillment of a dream long deferred. A woman had never been nominated to the Supreme Court, and women had not even been allowed to become lawyers until some one hundred years ago.

The historic announcement had its origins in March when Associate Justice Potter Stewart told Vice-President George Bush that he intended to retire. He had been appointed to the Court by President Eisenhower and had served for twenty-three years. The Reagan administration had three months before the public announcement of his retirement to search for a replacement. From the beginning the search focused on women.

Ronald Reagan had not been popular with women during his 1980 campaign. The polls showed that the majority of women did not intend to vote for him. In May 35 percent of women favored Reagan and 53 percent favored Carter. The Republican platform opposed the Equal Rights Amendment, Reagan opposed abortion, and many women perceived him as a warmonger.

His political advisers suggested he make a significant promise to women. So at a Los Angeles press conference in October 1980 he pledged that a woman would fill one of "the first [Supreme Court] vacancies in my administration." Shortly thereafter, the polls showed that his standing among women had improved.

Just as the political timing was right for the promise, the historical timing was right for the nomination of a woman to the Supreme Court. A small pool of experienced, qualified women candidates existed because, in the decade before, more women had been elected or appointed as judges. A new generation of women lawyers was coming out of law school. In fact, 10 percent of lawyers in 1981 were women, and 1 percent of federal judges were women. They were small percentages still, but they had increased greatly in just ten years.

Women's groups had been pushing for a woman Supreme Court justice for more than a decade. They had reminded and nagged and generally planted the idea in the public's mind. In 1965 they endorsed three women for the vacancy President Johnson filled with an old friend, Abe Fortas. In 1970 the National Women's Political Caucus said it was unhappy that a woman had not been nominated when Nixon appointed Justices Powell and Rehnquist. (Sandra O'Connor had also lamented that the President's nominee "does not wear a skirt.") In 1975 the National Organization of Women opposed the nomination of Justice Stevens because they said President Ford "owes us a duty" of a representative on the court.

The message finally got across to President Carter. There were no Supreme Court vacancies during his term, but he named forty women to federal judgeships. Until he did, only ten women had ever been federal judges.

By 1981, then, no one could argue that there were no qualified women around. The consciousnesses of the President and the public had been raised. Even the "Brethren" themselves were ready. Since 1971 there had been at least one woman law clerk assisting the justices. And they had dropped "Mr. Justice" as the preferred form of address. It became simply "Justice Burger," for example.

"I remember sitting with the first female circuit judge in history, Florence Allen," said former Justice Stewart. "Lawyers who wanted to be correct used to say, 'May it please the Court and Miss Allen,' which burned her up."

Despite his campaign promise, Reagan's record after the election had been unimpressive. He had appointed only one woman, Jeane Kirkpatrick (ambassador to the United Nations), to a cabinet-level post. Only one of the forty-one federal judges he had appointed was a woman.

When Reagan learned of Stewart's intention to resign, he remembered his promise to appoint a woman. Attorney General William French Smith and White House counsel Fred Fielding began making lists of the people Reagan should consider. Each of the two lists had about twenty-five names, and O'Connor's name was on both.

Judge O'Connor had several things going for her. She knew Chief Justice Burger, and she was a good friend of Justice William Rehnquist. Her name was suggested by at least one Arizona congressman. She had maintained strong ties with Stanford, and influential people from Stanford also recommended her to Smith.

Her qualifications were outstanding. She was thoroughly Republican, with the solid support of a conservative senator, Barry Goldwater of Arizona. Her views on law and order, the family, the death penalty, federalism, busing, and the separation of lawmaking from law-interpreting seemed consistent with the President's. She had been elected to a state legislature, which is rare for a Supreme Court justice, and she had served on the front lines as a trial judge in a city with one of the highest crime rates in the nation. She seemed to have no enemies.

By late June, the list of candidates had been narrowed to four women: O'Connor; Cornelia Kennedy, a judge on the Sixth U.S. Circuit Court of Appeals in Michigan; Mary Coleman, chief justice of the Michigan Supreme Court; and Amalya L. Kearse, a judge on the Second Circuit Court of Appeals in New York.

On June 25 O'Connor received her first inkling that she was being seriously considered. Attorney General Smith called to invite her to have dinner with him in Washington "to discuss the Potter Stewart vacancy." Before she went, a Justice Department lawyer was sent to Phoenix to gather more background information. Then two department lawyers interviewed her at home.

The Justice Department lawyers were charmed

when Sandra excused herself from the long questioning to prepare a salmon salad lunch. More important, however, they were impressed "by her intelligence and lawyerlike abilities."

Giving a cover story to her fellow judges, O'Connor then flew to Washington. Early on Tuesday, June 30, she had breakfast with Attorney General Smith. They met at the L'Enfant Plaza Hotel, so as not to attract reporters' attention. Later that day she endured ninety minutes of questioning by the White House staff. "We were testing her psychological and intellectual stamina, the lack of which has caused some justices to desert their conservative base," said one staff member. Her stamina has never been much in doubt since then.

Having passed those tests, O'Connor was summoned for an interview with Reagan. Sandra brought with her to that meeting all the social and political skills she had mastered so thoroughly in her public life. She reminded Reagan that they had met before, when he was the governor of California and she was an Arizona state senator. Both California and Arizona had been thinking of putting limits on state spending. Reagan wryly remembered: "Yours passed, but mine didn't."

In the forty-five minute conversation that followed Reagan became convinced that O'Connor should be his nominee. In political philosophy and on important issues her views seemed similar to his. To top it off, she shared his western upbringing and love of ranch life. "As far as I'm concerned," she told him, "the best place in the world to be is on a good cutting horse working cattle." After their meeting, Reagan told his staff he wasn't interested in interviewing anyone else.

Sandra returned to Arizona for a weekend in the mountains with heady thoughts edging out the usual Fourth of July celebrations. Clearly she was being seriously considered as Reagan's nominee to the vacancy on the Supreme Court. But she told friends on Saturday that she thought the chance of her appointment was remote, partly because her background was so similar to that of Associate Justice William Rehnquist. Maybe she didn't dare hope.

Before actually announcing his choice, Reagan decided to float O'Connor's name in public by having his staff drop a hint to the *Washington Post*. The next day the newspaper reported that Sandra Day O'Connor's name was at the top of a "short list" of possible nominees.

The reaction came quickly. The New Right and the Moral Majority flooded the White House with telegrams opposing the nomination, claiming O'Connor had a pro-abortion voting record in the Arizona legislature and was soft on some social issues. Reagan decided to stick with his candidate. Then he made the phone call to Phoenix.

When the nomination was officially announced on July 7, the public reaction was quite different. It was overwhelmingly positive and came from people with widely differing views. "Everybody's fallen in love with her," said Senator Goldwater. "When a candidate is endorsed by Ted Kennedy and Barry Goldwater, there's got to be something good about her." An AP–NBC

News poll showed that by the end of July only 6 percent of the adults interviewed opposed her nomination.

Women were especially pleased. Eleanor Smeal, president of the National Organization for Women, said the choice was "a major victory for women's rights." The National Women's Political Caucus celebrated the nomination as proof that "women are breaking the barriers of nearly two hundred years of exclusion from decision-making in our nation."

Engulfed as she was by the sudden wave of fame and popularity, Judge O'Connor still had work to do. Not only must she finish writing opinions for the court of appeals, but she must also prepare for the confirmation hearings that were to begin on September 9 before the Senate Judiciary Committee. The hearings are the main obstacle to a nominee's confirmation. They had proved troublesome for several recent nominees (Abe Fortas, Harrold Carswell, and Clement Haynsworth). Each senator on the committee would question her about the Constitution and recent issues before the Supreme Court.

Her fellow appeals court judges pitched in to help by taking some of her work themselves. She tried to settle down to what she does so well: preparing. She hired a staff to prepare in-depth background material on every possible question the senators could ask. She spent three weeks reading and digesting pages and pages of recent Supreme Court decisions and transcripts from other confirmation hearings.

While she was reading, Sandra was the object of

intense investigations by the FBI, the American Bar Association, and the staff of the Senate Judiciary Committee. She was also constantly interrupted by phone calls, even through the night, until the O'Connors left the phone off the hook and then got an unlisted number. Finally life in Phoenix became too hectic. On September 1 she left to hide away in an apartment in Washington.

As a result of organization and hard work, Sandra Day O'Connor was ready when the television cameras began to whir at 10:10 A.M., Wednesday, September 9. She had spent two days rehearsing with Justice Department officials, and she clearly had her answers and her nerves ready. "I really wasn't nervous," she would say later with aplomb. "I found the proceedings very fascinating."

Dressed in a tailored violet suit with a soft blouse, O'Connor sat through twenty-three opening statements before giving her own. She said that she was honored to be the first woman nominated a Supreme Court justice. "I happily share the honor with millions of American women of yesterday and today whose abilities and whose conduct have given me this opportunity for service."

Then she described her appreciation of the states' role in the federal system, the separate and distinct roles of the three branches of government, and the proper role of the judiciary, which she said was to interpret and apply the law. She warned that she could not tell the committee how she might vote on particular issues that might come before the Court and that she would not endorse or criticize decisions already made. It was a judicially correct position, but it also allowed her to avoid being drawn into controversy.

Next she proudly introduced her family: her husband John, her three sons, her sister, and her brother-in-law. She was the only Supreme Court nominee ever to have four years of "homemaking and child care" in her biography.

Then began the serious questions. For the next three days questions came on many subjects—busing, the death penalty, the ERA, minority rights—and O'Connor handled them all. She was calm, cool, and controlled throughout.

The most persistent questioning came on abortion, judicial activism, and access to the federal courts. The only real opposition came on the issue of abortion. The Supreme Court had made a landmark decision in 1973, *Roe* v. *Wade*, which limited the states' right to regulate abortion. In the majority opinion, Justice Blackmun wrote that the Court "has recognized that a right of personal privacy . . . does exist under the Constitution" and that a woman has a right to terminate her pregnancy if she so chooses. He said the state could step in during the second trimester of a pregnancy, to protect the mother's health, and in the third trimester, to protect the health of the fetus while not endangering the health of the mother.

Anti-abortion advocates have been seeking a reversal of that decision. They want the states to be allowed fully to restrict abortion. They feared that O'Connor would not vote their way on the Court. They were concerned about several of her votes in the Arizona legislature: a 1970 vote in committee to repeal Arizona's law prohibiting abortion; her support of the 1973 family planning bill, which would have made birth control methods and information available to anyone who requested it; her 1974 opposition to a University of Arizona stadium bond issue that had a rider banning state abortion funding for the university hospital; and her vote against House Concurrent Memorial No. 2002, in 1974, in which the Arizona legislature called on Congress to pass a constitutional amendment allowing the states to prohibit abortion. (See Chapter 5.)

O'Connor explained her reasons for each vote. They varied from a belief that Arizona's abortion law was too broad to a conviction that constitutional amendments should not be undertaken hastily. Personally, she had held an "abhorrence of abortion as a remedy" for a long time, she said. "It is a practice in which I would not have engaged." She also stated candidly, however, that "I'm over the hill. I'm not going to be pregnant any more, so perhaps it's easy for me to speak."

Her answers left her vote on any future abortion case in doubt. In general she seemed very cautious about legislation on abortion. Senator Jeremiah Denton of Alabama became quite frustrated after thirty minutes of questioning O'Connor on the subject. When asked by Chairman Strom Thurmond if he wanted another fifteen minutes, he replied, "I don't know whether another month would do." Abortion foes were far from happy over her responses, but it was clear that a majority of the senators would not allow the nomination to be sidetracked by that single issue.

Persistent questions also came on O'Connor's judicial philosophy. The Warren Court, which preceded the Burger Court, was generally regarded as an activist court, one that went beyond narrow interpretations of the Constitution if it felt that was necessary to correct injustices. One example of such judicial activism was the 1954 *Brown* decision, which found that segregated school systems are unconstitutional.

Chief Justice Burger and recent Republican Presidents have tried to change the Court so that it uses more restraint and does not try to make social policy. Conservative senators were looking for evidence that O'Connor believed in judicial restraint rather than judicial activism.

O'Connor testified that her experience in the state legislature helped her recognize the necessity for judicial restraint. "I know well the difference between a legislator and a judge, and the role of the judge is to interpret the law, not make it," she reassured them.

One liberal Democrat, Senator Howard M. Metzenbaum of Ohio, was disturbed by what she had written in the *William and Mary Law Review* article. Under a civil rights law passed after the Civil War, defendants who claim that their civil rights have been violated by an officer of the state may bring their cases to the attention of the federal courts. O'Connor had suggested that access to the federal courts for convicted defendants should be more restricted.

Metzenbaum had successfully sponsored a bill to give them more access by removing a requirement that at least $10,000 be involved in the dispute. "You seem to think that was a bad idea," he said. O'Connor responded by stressing her faith in a "strong and capable state court system" that is willing and able to protect individuals' federal rights. Her faith in the state courts would be demonstrated in some of the decisions she made the first year.

Representatives of many women's organizations testified at the hearings, and all were pleased at the nomination. O'Connor was seen as supportive of many women's issues, particularly wage discrimination and property rights, but she was not portrayed as a leader of the troops. When Delaware Senator Joseph Biden urged her to be more than just another justice, saying, "You have an obligation . . . to women in this country to speak out on those issues" when you can, the audience burst into applause, but O'Connor remained silent. The hope of women's groups was that having a woman on the Court would make more than just a symbolic difference.

One of the most influential groups in the approval of Supreme Court nominees is the American Bar Association, the national professional organization of lawyers. Its Standing Committee on the Federal Judiciary investigates and then rates every nominee for a federal judgeship. Since its creation in 1948, the committee had been all male, and it had tended to give women candidates lower ratings. But when it was time for the committee's recommendation, a woman rose to give the report. She was its chairperson, Brooksley Landau, who said the committee had found O'Connor "Qualified." O'Connor met "the highest standards of judicial temperament and integrity." Landau said it had been difficult to judge whether O'Connor met "the highest standards of professional competence" (the rating it had given Justice Stevens) because she did not have federal judicial experience.

The ABA could not be more professionally enthusiastic, but that was no surprise given the fact that O'Connor did not have a national reputation. She was little known outside of Arizona and only once had served on a national governmental board, the National Defense Advisory Commission on Women in Service. At least one senator thought her rural roots would be a breath of fresh air on the Court.

By the end of the hearings, most people still did not know how Justice O'Connor would function on the Supreme Court. She had given a masterful performance, but her performance was as much style as substance. She had demonstrated her celebrated "cool." *Time* magazine described her as "probably the most thoroughly prepared nominee in history," and Senator Goldwater noted that she cited Supreme Court opinions "as easily as most people would recite their birthdates."

Throughout she seemed very sure of herself and of her role. Asked how she wanted to be remembered in history, O'Connor laughed and said, "The tombstone question—what do I want on the tombstone?" to which she replied, "I hope it might say, 'Here lies a good judge.'"

She prevailed, too, by refusing to comment on issues that might come before the Court again, and no senator was able or willing to push her beyond that. Her answers were often just descriptions of the state of the law and of past decisions. One legal scholar described her appearance as "stonewalling."

Unable to pinpoint her views, supporters and detractors alike came to their own conclusions. Senator John East decided that she would have joined the dissent in _Roe_ v. _Wade_. Columnist Ellen Goodman concluded that she was "as much of a conservative as you can find in a qualified woman and as much of a feminist as you can find in a conservative."

Despite the committee's attempt to judge her qualifications, it would have been virtually impossible to oppose the first woman nominee to the Court. "If anything happened to O'Connor on her way to the Supreme Court," wrote columnist Mary McGrory, "the women of America would storm the Senate Judiciary Committee and trash it."

From the beginning the hearings reverberated with celebration. Large sections of the hearing room were packed with spectators, and television cameras were stationed outside the room and outside on the Capitol steps. O'Connor came down the aisle the first day on the arm of a courtly

Senator Strom Thurmond. Teas and lunches were sandwiched in during recesses. Everyone was quite adulatory. Only one male chauvinist was heard from. A private citizen from Washington, D.C., grumbled in a letter put in the hearing transcript that "The hard fact is: Mrs. O'Connor is putting another man out of work."

When the last word was in, the committee recessed for the weekend and returned on Tuesday to vote on the confirmation. By then even the New Right senators wanted to support the President. The vote was 17–0 in favor of confirmation with Jeremiah Denton voting present, neither for nor against.

A week later it was the whole Senate's turn to heap praise on O'Connor. For four hours, speeches were made to a nearly empty chamber, and at 6:00 P.M. the vote was taken. A nervous O'Connor wrung her hands and waited in an anteroom near the Senate floor. "This is the longest five minutes of my life," she said but her worry was unnecessary. The vote was unanimous, 99–0 (one senator was absent).

Her longtime friend and champion Barry Goldwater let out a joyful "Hear! Hear!" in the Senate chamber. A few minutes later he gave her a hug. Then Vice-President Bush, Attorney General Smith, and several senators appeared with Justice O'Connor on the steps of the Capitol, which faces the Supreme Court building over an expanse of green.

"My hope is that ten years from now, after I've been across the street at work for a while, they'll all be glad they gave me that wonderful vote," she told the cheering onlookers. She also said she was "absolutely overjoyed."

O'Connor was the toast of Washington. That night at a candlelit dinner given by the Thurmonds, the new justice quipped that "Thomas Jefferson and James Madison would be turning over in their graves right now, but let's hope Abigail Adams would be pleased."

Except for the celebrating, the swearing in, and the moving, the appointment process was over. For Justice O'Connor the work had just begun.

# 8

# Her Honor,
# Justice O'Connor

The Supreme Court Building in Washington, D.C., is an awe-inspiring structure, as befits the work of the nine justices within. Made of white marble with two large wings on either side, it occupies an entire block. The center front is flanked by statues of Justice. The portico is supported by sixteen Corinthian columns and bears the inscription, "Equal Justice under Law." One must climb a long flight of wide, stone steps to reach the formal main door. It is hardly human size.

Sandra O'Connor must have felt a sense of awe the first Monday in October as she started the 1981–1982 term. She arrived shortly before 8:00 A.M., driving a compact car, to hear the year's first oral arguments, the presentations made by lawyers who are trying to persuade the justices to decide in their favor. "The nature of the responsibility is such that it is not a task that anyone can approach with anything but awe," she had commented before leaving Phoenix.

Justice O'Connor had already been at work for a week. She had moved into an office next to Justice Rehnquist's, adding her own American Indian art and plants to the legal volumes, leather chairs, and fireplace. She and her fellow justices had spent the week in conference, deciding which of some one thousand appeals that had arrived since June they would accept for a decision that term. Despite a week's experience, she still found herself getting lost as she navigated the cavernous halls.

The first Monday in October is the formal beginning of the term, however, and spectators had lined up all the way down the front steps to be present on O'Connor's first day, October 5. When all were seated in the courtroom, O'Connor filed out of the robing room with the other justices and took her place to the far left of the half-hexagon-shaped table. She looked "small but undaunted," according to one observer. John O'Connor was sitting in front as the formal business began, appropriately enough, with the admission of three women to practice before the Supreme Court.

As the cases were argued, the justices interrupted nervous lawyers many times with questions about their reasoning or interpretation of the law. Several times O'Connor put on her glasses to scan the briefs she had already read. One case involving the controversial secretary of the interior, James Watt, elicited her first question.

At the end of the session, the justices all shook hands with one another and returned to their chambers and desks loaded with paperwork. The

Court hears a total of 168 hours of oral argument each term, leaving the rest of the time for writing. In case conferences on Friday they discuss the cases heard, and each justice indicates how he or she will vote. Then each opinion is assigned to a justice to write.

Once an opinion is written, it is circulated to the other justices and each may make suggestions or indicate whether she or he will join that opinion. The justices may discuss the cases with each other further, but most of the communicating is done in writing. Justice Stewart has described the work as grueling. After several months on the job, Justice O'Connor agreed that she didn't know anything that could adequately prepare someone for the life of a Supreme Court justice.

By the time O'Connor received her first writing assignment, she was well into a working routine. Her attempt to organize an exercise class for women at the Court fizzled, so she started stopping at a Georgetown exercise salon each morning at six-thirty. Many mornings she had already been up for a couple of hours reading briefs, the legal documents lawyers prepare on their cases.

When she arrived at work, her "in box" was full, and it would fill again three more times each day. She might not leave her desk until 8:00 P.M., which left little time for gourmet cooking or dancing. Her long hours paid off, however, because she was regarded as well prepared and alert at oral arguments and assertive at case conferences, asking questions that went to the heart of the issues.

Much was new in Sandra's life all at once: a new city (with no open skies), new social acquaintances, new jobs for herself and John, and new colleagues. Deciding to move had not been hard. Sandra, at age fifty-one, was at a point in her life when she could move. "I didn't have to concern myself with the children because they are all at an age when they are in college or working."

John was fully behind the move, too, although it required him to find a new job at the peak of his career. He said the decision was really very simple. "Sandra and I have been married for twenty-nine years. We want to continue to live together." John joined the Washington law firm of Miller-Chevalier, which specializes in federal tax matters and does not have frequent cases before the Supreme Court.

They moved from the home their children had grown up in to an apartment in Washington. Sandra's new job left her little time to worry about household management. "All they've got in the place is four chairs and two beds," her brother Alan said early in the year. She was seen unloading one U-Haul, but she had no time at first to cook or hire a housekeeper.

The need to staff her office at the Court was more important than furnishing the apartment. She retained the three clerks Potter Stewart had hired and added a fourth from her husband's Phoenix law firm, Ruth McGregor. She brought a secretary with her from Arizona and hired other personnel.

The extra staff was certainly needed. The new

While serving as a state court judge, O'Connor also became a trustee of Stanford University. (Photo: Stanford University)

On the day she was nominated to the Supreme Court by President Reagan, Judge O'Connor introduced to the press at a packed news conference in Phoenix her husband John and her three sons (left to right): Jay, Brian, and Scott. (Photo: Don B. Stevenson/Mesa Tribune)

The nomination put O'Connor in the public spotlight and high on the list of Most Admired Women. Here she gives the commencement address at her son Brian's graduation from Colorado College. The task was difficult, she said, because "everyone knows a mother just doesn't know what she is talking about." (Photo: Ken Abbott Photos)

Before the 1982–1983 term began, John and Sandra enjoyed an evening of dancing at the Wolf Trap Center Associates Ball. They won the door prize—a trip to Morocco. (Photo: Wolf Trap Center Associates)

John O'Connor held the Bibles as Sandra Day O'Connor was sworn in by Chief Justice Warren Burger as the first woman justice on the Supreme Court. At this private ceremony before the public ceremony, she took the judicial oath to "administer justice without respect to persons, and do equal right to the poor and the rich." (Photo: Michael Evans/The White House)

The new justice descends the steps of the Supreme Court building with Chief Justice Burger after the public swearing-in ceremony, September 25, 1981. (Photo: Wide World)

justice was overwhelmed with congratulations. While job hunting, John pitched in to help send out four thousand replies to the mail she had received. One unusual gift was a T-shirt sent from the Woman's Law Caucus of Northern Kentucky University's Chase Law School. The T-shirt depicted one woman justice and her eight male colleagues, with the comment, "One down, eight to go."

O'Connor replied, "The T-shirt is terrific. Forgive me if I don't wear it around my colleagues just yet, but it will be nice to get some female companions in the future." She continued to support women in law and was pleased that five women had applied for the judgeship she had vacated in Arizona.

Both of the O'Connors were moved by the effect that her nomination had. "I had no idea when I was appointed how much it would mean to many people around the country," she said. She responded conscientiously to all who wrote to her, including the parents of a promising young student who had committed suicide. Later in the year when she gave the commencement address at her son Brian's graduation from Colorado College, she addressed her comments to young people, encouraging them to think about creativity, work, the individual, and love. People seemed to respond to both the success and the maternal elements in her life.

During their first two months in Washington, the O'Connors kept up a heavy social schedule, too. They were feted at a farewell dinner attended by 850 in Phoenix in November, and they were welcomed to the social circles of the capital with many dinners. Sandra was recognized almost everywhere she went—including the supermarket—and besieged by requests for interviews and photo sessions. She could do little without attracting public attention. By December, however, the O'Connors were staying home in the evenings. The workload of the Supreme Court demanded it.

Being the only woman on a court was nothing new to Sandra, but getting to know the views of eight other justices at once was a challenge. Except for Rehnquist and Burger, she knew them only by reputation. Three of the justices—William Brennan, Thurgood Marshall, and Byron White—had served on the Court when Earl Warren was chief justice. Brennan and Marshall had been part of a fairly liberal majority then, but they were now a liberal minority of two.

The Burger Court, so called since Warren Burger was appointed chief justice in 1969, was more conservative. Its two most conservative members were Burger and Rehnquist. The four other justices—White, Lewis Powell, Harry Blackmun, and John Paul Stevens—were part of a shifting center. They were generally moderate in their views but sometimes liberal and sometimes conservative.

Most people expected that Sandra O'Connor would be part of the shifting center, too, although she leaned toward the conservative. Seven of the other eight justices had served together for more

than ten years, but they had not become very con-
vivial, either ideologically or socially. They had a
hard time agreeing on major issues, and they had
been described as being "in chronic disagree-
ment." There had been many 5–4 decisions, in
which the vote of one justice could change the
outcome. O'Connor's one vote was not expected
to make a significant difference on most issues.
Some hoped that her experience in encouraging
compromise as a majority leader might help bring
the justices closer.

During the 1981–1982 term, the Court faced a
number of significant issues: school busing, the
death penalty, child pornography, removal of
books from school libraries, affirmative action, the
education of the children of illegal aliens, and the
constitutionality of Carter's energy program. By
Christmas vacation, the Court had agreed to hear
152 cases or sets of cases. The year's work was cut
out.

Sandra's first assignment was to write the
majority opinion in *Watt* v. *Energy Action*. It was
not a difficult opinion because all nine justices
agreed that Secretary Watt was acting within the
Constitution in administering the Outer Continental Shelf Lands Act Amendments. The justices
said the Energy Action Educational Foundation
could not sue Watt for not carrying out a provision
of the law because they had not been "injured"
by Watt's action. Whether Watt was carrying out
the law properly was a matter for Congress to decide.

The next O'Connor opinion, *Rose* v. *Lundy*, revealed more of her judicial philosophy. It was a complicated case in criminal law that involved the writ of habeas corpus. The Great Writ, as it is called, provides a means by which state prison inmates can gain release if they can prove that their federal constitutional rights were violated.

The Court decided that Lundy had not done all he could in state courts before he appealed to the federal court. O'Connor thought the state courts should be given an opportunity to respond to each of his complaints first. She outlined a "total exhaustion" rule: Lundy had to present all of his claims to the state courts before going to federal court.

The *Rose* opinion was difficult; it took five months to gain agreement from the justices. Although the final tally was 8–1, the majority was fragmented. Some justices agreed with parts of O'Connor's opinion but not others.

In two other opinions she wrote the first year— *Engle* v. *Isaac* and *U.S.* v. *Frady*—O'Connor amplified her views on the writ of habeas corpus. In both decisions, the Court made it more difficult for a prisoner to win a new trial, a different sentence, or even freedom by persuading a federal court that his or her constitutional rights had been violated during the trial.

A majority of the justices supported both opinions, and O'Connor became an important voice in limiting prisoners' access to the federal courts. The decisions were part of a conservative trend by the Court to back the arguments of the police, prosecutors, and state judges and reject those of defendants.

As the year wore on and more decisions were released, O'Connor's conservatism became more obvious. She was a strong advocate for the new federalism—the return of power and responsibility to the states and local officials. In her dissent on *Federal Energy Regulatory Commission* v. *Mississippi*, she argued that state legislatures and agencies should not be considered "field offices of the national bureaucracy." She said President Carter's energy program interfered with the regulation of public utilities, which had always been the states' job. In a case involving the use of water from wells in the dry western state of Nevada, O'Connor sided with the state's right, in joining Rehnquist's dissent.

Two of the most interesting O'Connor opinions involved claims of sex discrimination. The first— *Ford Motor Company* v. *Equal Employment Opportunity Commission*—concerned three women who had sued Ford under Title VII of the Civil Rights Act of 1964. The women had applied for a job at the Ford warehouse in Charlotte, North Carolina. Men were hired for the job, and the women claimed Ford had discriminated against them in hiring. No woman had ever worked at the job they applied for in the Ford warehouse at that time. Ford wanted to settle the case by offering the women jobs, without retroactive seniority and back pay. The women felt the offer was not enough.

In a rather pragmatic opinion, O'Connor said the job offer was sufficient. The person discriminated against mainly needs a job, she reasoned, and can't expect to get everything by suing.

Moreover, the employer needed a good reason for hiring someone it had once discriminated against. The incentive in this case would be having the suit dropped. Her opinion in this case was based on interpretation of a law passed by Congress.

In the second case—*Mississippi University for Women* v. *Hogan* —O'Connor found unconstitutional sex discrimination. Her opinion was based on an interpretation of the Constitution. Joe Hogan was a nurse who wanted to gain additional training. He applied to a program in the School of Nursing at Mississippi University for Women, which was located in his hometown. He was denied admission because he was male. Mississippi University for Women is the oldest all-female public university in the country.

O'Connor said the discrimination against him was unconstitutional under the equal protection clause of the Fourteenth Amendment. Laws that treat men and women differently are constitutional, she said, only if there is an "exceedingly persuasive justification" for the different treatment. Such sex differentiation could not be justified in this case. Instead, the policy "tends to perpetuate the stereotyped view of nursing as exclusively a women's job," she wrote.

A footnote in her opinion caught one reporter's eye. In it O'Connor quoted the Court in its 1872 decision that Myra Bradwell could not become a lawyer. The Court had talked of the "peculiar characteristics, destiny and mission of woman." Clearly O'Connor had something to say about the destiny and mission of women.

Other decisions indicate what O'Connor's long-term effect on the court might be. (At age fifty-three she is twenty years younger than many of the other justices, and her influence will endure.) She thought the death penalty was constitutional, but she wanted to be sure all possible consideration had been given the defendant. She generally favored open government: keeping trials open to the press and making government agencies' information available to the public. She upheld Indian tribes in their attempts to tax the oil and gas that were obtained from their reservations. She tended to stick close to the intent of Congress when interpreting a law. She generally voted in favor of the states' rights to regulate the use of their resources.

In affirmative action and voting rights cases she required proof of the intent to discriminate. Proving intent is harder than just showing the discriminatory effect of a policy. O'Connor may take a similar position on school desegregation cases.

In all, O'Connor wrote thirteen opinions. They were described as no-nonsense, clear, practical, and unambiguous. She dissented from the majority in twenty-two cases. She did not agree with the majority when it ruled that Texas must pay for the education of the children of illegal aliens in the state, that a school board cannot remove books from a school library, and that Washington state's anti-busing initiative was unconstitutional.

In a large number of decisions—123 out of 139—she voted the same as Justice Rehnquist. People began calling them "the Arizona twins," just as Justices Burger and Blackmun were called "the Minnesota twins." Both came from Minnesota and tended to vote alike when Blackmun joined the Court in 1970, but Justice Blackmun soon became more independent and liberal in his views. O'Connor is expected to be more independent in her views than Rehnquist, who is consistently conservative. O'Connor, however, generally seemed more conservative than some had thought she would be.

Women hoped that her role on the Court would not be merely that of a token woman, that her experience as a homemaker and community volunteer would add a unique perspective. Her husband John commented that her sense of priorities—family first—"is much more important to the court than any degree of competence she may have." A writer in *Ms. Magazine* hoped that she would breathe "real life" into the deliberations that concern women and the family. Justice O'Connor wrote in the *Mississippi University for Women* case that the Court should use "reasoned analysis" in cases pertaining to women rather than "the mechanical application of traditional, often inaccurate, assumptions about the proper roles of men and women."

The Burger Court had been rather traditional in its views of women. Justice Marshall once commented that the majority of the justices are "a bunch of rich, old white men incapable of understanding what life is like for those who are black and/or poor and/or female." O'Connor would relieve one of those deficiencies.

Poor she is not. Financial statements released during her first year on the Court showed that the O'Connors are millionaires. Among the justices, they were second in wealth only to the Powells. Some of their wealth derives, of course, from a two-lawyer, two-income family. But it may be a barrier of the type Justice Marshall described. O'Connor's position as a woman justice made her nontraditional by definition, but other characteristics of her life made her more a part of the brethren than the sisterhood, as one magazine commented.

Throughout her first few years, until more women are appointed to the Court, O'Connor can expect to be in the spotlight. She is bound to be measured as the first woman, just as Roger Taney, Louis Brandeis, and Marshall were measured as the first Catholic, the first Jew, and the first black, respectively. She will have a unique burden, and every major decision she makes will be closely watched. "If she is superior she will help the next generation of women, but she will be judged more harshly than men," said Jill Wine Banks, a former Watergate prosecutor.

She handled the spotlight very well the first year, maintaining her skill with deadpan humor. Arriving late at one gathering early in the year she offered the excuse that she had been busy "filming next week's edition of 'What's My Line.'"

Her first year gave a mere glimpse of how she would vote on issues particularly affecting women. Abortion, the most troublesome issue, did not arise in a case her first term. She seemed strong on women's constitutional rights but deferred to the intent of Congress in cases that were based on a law like the Civil Rights Act of 1964. Being on the bench has been described as a self-discovery process, and the process is not complete in one year.

The Court recessed for the summer at the beginning of July, and Sandra left Washington to deliver commencement speeches and to travel to Africa, Arizona, and a Stanford reunion. The summer continued the celebration of an amazing year.

Sandra O'Connor is a woman at the height of her life. She is trim, well-dressed, and attractive, with wavy hair, heavy eyebrows, smile lines around her eyes and mouth, a tanned face, and good posture. Her attractiveness is enhanced by her power. She occupies on the Court what has been regarded as the citadel of the lawyer's profession.

O'Connor cannot help inspiring other women because she fought the same battles, in her own style. She overcame a prejudice against admitting women to law school, against hiring them as lawyers once they graduate, against hiring them for part-time jobs during their child-rearing years, and against electing a woman as a leader, and she also experienced the loneliness of being the only or the first woman in many situations.

She had advantages not available to all: intelligence, good parents, a top-notch education, and a supportive husband with the income to facilitate her efforts. But she added to that determination her own hard work, rational goal-setting, and the will to succeed. Above all, she believed in the American dream: that any person can be—well, if not President, then a Supreme Court justice.

# Sources

Following are some of the most important sources of information for each chapter.

### Introduction, Chapters 1 and 2
Interviews with Sandra Day O'Connor, Ada Mae Wilkey Day, Henry (Harry) A. Day, H. Alan Day, Ann Day Alexander, Flournoy Davis Manzo.

Correspondence with Laura Kramer, historian at the Radford School.

"Sandra Day O'Connor: First Woman on Our Highest Court," Prudence Mackintosh, *McCall's*, October 1982, p. 12.

"Sandra Day O'Connor of Arizona: Portrait of the Justice as a Young Woman," Garry Clifford and James R. Gaines, *People*, October 12, 1981, pp. 46–51.

"Justice Sandra Day O'Connor: Reflections of a Fellow Jurist," Laurance T. Wren, *Arizona State Law Journal*, Summer 1981, pp. 647–648.

### Chapters 3 and 4
Interviews with Beatrice Challis Laws, Calista Farrell Handwerg, Marilyn Schwartz Brown, Fred Steiner, John B.

Hurlbut, Lowell Turrentine, Harry John Rathbun, Thomas H. Tobin, Gary K. Nelson, William E. Eubank, Ann Day Alexander, Jackie McNulty, Jackie Steiner, Darrell Smith, Sandra Day O'Connor.

Correspondence with Kay Daley, Stanford Alumni Association editor, and Keith Sorenson.

The *Arizona Republic* and the *Phoenix Gazette*, articles throughout 1957–69.

### Chapters 5 and 6

Interviews with William Jacquin, Eino M. Jacobson, John Foreman, Tom Henze, William E. Eubank, Jackie Steiner, Alice L. Bendheim, Ann Day Alexander.

"Nomination of Sandra Day O'Connor," Hearings before the Committee on the Judiciary, U.S. Senate, September 9–11, 1981.

"Sandra," Dickson Hartwell, *Phoenix*, February 1971.

"O'Connor: Flexible . . . and Tough," Ruth Marcus and David F. Pike, *National Law Journal*, July 20, 1981.

"Trends in the Relationship between the Federal and State Courts from the Perspective of a State Court Judge," Sandra Day O'Connor, *William and Mary Law Review*, Summer 1981, p. 4.

Wren, *op. cit.*

The *Arizona Republic*, the *Phoenix Gazette*, articles throughout 1969–82; the *Washington Post*, articles throughout 1981–82.

### Chapter 7

"Women as Supreme Court Candidates, from Florence Allen to Sandra Day O'Connor," Beverly B. Cook, *Judicature*, December-January 1982, p. 6.

Epstein, Cynthia Fuchs. *Women in Law*, New York: Basic Books, 1981.

The *Arizona Republic*, the *New York Times*, the *Washington Post*, *Newsweek*, *Time*, *U.S. News & World Report*, articles throughout 1981–82.

**Chapter 8**

Interview with Sandra Day O'Connor.

Slip opinions of Supreme Court decisions, 1981–82 term.

Articles by Linda Greenhouse in the *New York Times* and by Elder Witt in *Congressional Quarterly*, 1981–82.

Goode, Stephen. *The Controversial Court*, New York: Julian Messner, 1982.

"The Supreme Court of the United States," Supreme Court Historical Society, and correspondence with Betsy T. Strawderman, assistant curator, Supreme Court of the United States.

"Justice," Nina Totenberg, *Working Woman*, September 1981, pp. 80–82.

"Sandra O'Connor and the Supremes," Lynn Hecht Schafran, *Ms. Magazine*, October 1981, p. 71.

"One Step at a Time . . . and Keep Walking," Sandra Day O'Connor, Commencement Address at Colorado College, May 31, 1982.

"Sandra Day O'Connor, Warm, Witty, and Wise," Pam Hait, *Ladies' Home Journal*, April 1982, p. 40.

# Index

## A

Abortion, 56, 79, 84, 87–88, 113
Affirmative action, 107, 111
Allen, Florence, 81
American Bar Association, 86, 90–91
Apache Indians, 4
Arizona, 2–10, 35–94

## B

Babbitt, Bruce, 71
Banks, Jill Wine, 113
Bar exam, 35
Bendheim, Alice, 56, 68
Biden, Joseph, 90
Blackmun, Harry, 106, 112
Bradwell, Myra, 110
Brandeis, Louis, 113
Brennan, William, 106
Burger, Warren, 76, 77, 81, 89, *103*, *104*, 106, 112

Burger Court, 106–114. *See also specific cases*
Burgess, Isabella, 49
Bush, George, 79
Busing, 54, 107, 111

## C

Carswell, Harrold, 85
Carter, Jimmy, 72, 79, 109
Challis, Beatrice, 23–24, 26–27
Child pornography, 107
Civil Rights Act, 1964, 48–49, 109, 114
Coleman, Mary, 82

## D

Day, Ada Mae, 2, 5–10, 15, 22, *38*, *40*
Day, Alan, 14, 15, 18
Day, Ann, 14, 42, 61
Day, Harry, 2, 3–10, 15, 22, *38*
Death penalty, 54, 69, 107, 111

Denton, Jeremiah, 88
Depression, 9
Discrimination, 109–110,
        111
Divorce, 67, 69–70
Drug possession, 70–71

# E

East, John, 92
Education, 54, 107, 111
Eisenhower, Dwight D.,
        79
Energy, 107, 109
Energy Action
        Educational
        Foundation, 107
*Engle v. Isaac*, 108
Equal Pay Act, 1963, 48
Equal Rights
        Amendment,
        54–55, 79
Eubank, William, 47

# F

Family planning, 54, 56,
        88
Fannin, Paul, 55
FBI, 86
*Federal Energy
        Regulatory
        Commission v.
        Mississippi*, 109
*Feminine Mystique, The*
        (Friedan), 42–43,
        48

Fielding, Fred, 81
Ford, Gerald, 80
*Ford Motor Company v.
        Equal
        Employment
        Opportunity
        Commission*, 109
Foreman, John, 68, 70–71
Fortas, Abe, 80, 85
Friedan, Betty, 42–43, 48

# G

Goldwater, Barry, 43, 45,
        46, 55, 82, 84, 91
Goodman, Ellen, 92
Great Writ, 108
Guitierrez, Alfredo, 59
Gun control, 53–54

# H

Hance, Margaret, 49, 79
Haynesworth, Clement,
        85
Henze, Tom, 69
Hufstedler, Shirley, 29

# J

Jacquin, William, 58
Johnson, Lyndon B., 80
Judicial activism, 89

# K

Kearse, Amalya L., 82
Kennedy, Cornelia, 82

Kennedy, Ted, 84
Kirkpatrick, Jeane, 81

# L

*Ladies' Home Journal*, 44
Landau, Brooksley, 91
Lockwood, Lorna, 49
Luce, Clare Boothe, 7

# M

McGregor, Ruth, 98
Marshall, Thurgood, 106,
    112, 113
Mead, Margaret, 57
Medicaid, 54
Metzenbaum, Howard
    M., 89–90
*Mississippi University for
    Women v. Hogan*,
    110
*Ms. Magazine*, 112

# N

National Association of
    Women Judges, 75
National Organization for
    Women (NOW), 49,
    80, 85
National Women's
    Political Caucus,
    1970, 80
Nixon, Richard, 80

# O

O'Connor, Brian, 42, 46,
    60, *100*, 105
O'Connor, Jay, 42, 46, 60,
    *100*
O'Connor, John III,
    27–28, 30–31,
    33–39, *40*, 70, 98,
    *100*, *102*, *103*, 105
O'Connor, Sandra Day,
    37, *39*, *40*, *99–104*
  on abortion, 56, 84, 87–
    88, 113
  on affirmative action,
    107, 111
  appearance, 52, 96, 114
  as Arizona judge, 65–76
  in Arizona legislature,
    51–63
  on busing, 54, 111
  childhood of, 1, 7–18
  conservatism of, 108–
    109, 112
  courtship and marriage,
    27–28, 30–31
  on death penalty, 54,
    69, 110
  on education, 54, 111
  on energy, 107, 109
  on family planning, 54,
    56, 88
  first law jobs, 29–31, 33,
    34, 39–50
  on gun control, 53–54
  on property laws,
    55–56, 90

on sex discrimination,
109–110
at Stanford University,
17–29
as Supreme Court
justice, 77–115
on tenant rights, 74
on voting rights, 111
as wife and mother,
33–50, 60–61, 87
on women's issues,
54–55, 57, 80, 84,
87–88, 90–91,
109–110, 112,
113–114
writings of, 73–74, 89
on writ of habeas
corpus, 108
O'Connor, Scott
Hampton, 36, 46,
60, *100*
Outer Continental Shelf
Lands Act
Amendments, 107

**P**

Perry, David J., 67
Phoenix, 35–94
Pollution, 54
Pornography, 107
Powell, Lewis, 106, 113
Property laws, 55–56, 90

**R**

Reagan, Ronald, 60, 77,
78, 79–80, 83, 84

Rehnquist, William, 25,
82, 84, 106, 111–
112
Report of the President's
Commission on the
Status of Women,
The, 1963, 48
*Roe v. Wade*, 87, 92
*Rose v. Lundy*, 107–108

**S**

*Saturday Evening Post*,
44
Sex discrimination,
109–110
Shroeder, Mary, 72
Smeal, Eleanor, 85
Smith, William French,
29, 81, 82, 83
Stanford, Leland, 19
*Stanford Law Review*, 25,
28
Stanford University, 17–
29
Stevens, John Paul, 106
Stewart, Potter, 79, 81, 98
Supreme Court, 77–115
procedure, 96–97
*See also specific cases*
Supreme Court Building,
Washington, D.C.,
95

**T**

Taney, Roger, 113
Tenant rights, 74

Thurmond, Strom, 88
*Time*, 91
Tobin, Tom, 39, 41

# U

United Nations, 81
*U.S. v. Frady*, 108

# V

Voting rights, 111

# W

Warren, Earl, 106
*Washington Post*, 84

Watt, James, 96, 107
*Watt v. Energy Action*,
    107
"What's My Line," 113
White, Byron, 106
Williams, John R., 49
Women's issues, 49,
    54–55, 57, 80, 84,
    87–88, 90–91,
    109–110, 112,
    113–114
Women's Movement, 49,
    57, 80
World War II, 19
Wren, Laurance T., 76, 78
Writ of habeas corpus,
    108

# About the Author

Judith Bentley is a graduate of Oberlin College and holds a master's degree in the History of American Civilization from New York University. She is a freelance writer who lives with her family in Bellevue, Washington. She writes on non-fiction topics of concern to young people, including busing, recent immigration, and national health care.